THE PREVENTION OF TERRORISM ACT

The Case for Repeal

Catherine Scorer and Patricia Hewitt

National Council for Civil Liberties
1981

Acknowledgements

We should like to thank Dermot Walsh for preparing the chapter on the operation of the Acts in Northern Ireland; Rick Hartog, for research assistance; Larry Grant for checking the draft; and Martin Flannery MP and Jo Richardson MP for assistance with Parliamentary Questions.

National Council for Civil Liberties
186 Kings Cross Road, London WC1X 9DE.

ISBN 0 901108 94 4

Printed and bound in Great Britain
by the Russell Press Ltd., Nottingham.

Contents

Preface

NCCL is utterly opposed to terrorist activity. We have consistently condemned those who have turned to assassinations and bombings in their desire to change or defend the present constitutional status of Northern Ireland.

Our opposition to terrorism is in no sense compromised by our opposition to laws such as the Prevention of Terrorism Act which were supposedly introduced to curb terrorist activity. Our position has often been misrepresented by those who believe that criticism of emergency legislation must imply support for the terrorists. Nothing could be further from the truth. We oppose emergency legislation because it diminishes the rights of *all* citizens by providing the Government, the police and the army with powers unchallengeable in the courts, and by corrupting the standards which are central to the administration of justice. NCCL opposes terrorism not only because terrorists threaten the lives of citizens, but because their activities provide the apparent justification for drastic curtailment of traditional liberties.

NCCL's concern with emergency legislation in Northern Ireland began in 1936, when we published the report of a Special Commission of Inquiry into the Special Powers Acts.* That report concluded:

> 'First, that through the operation of the Special Powers Acts contempt has been begotten for the representative institutions of government.
>
> 'Secondly, that through the use of Special Powers individual liberty is no longer protected by law, but is at the arbitrary disposition of the Executive. This abrogation of the rule of law has been so practised as to bring the freedom of the subject into contempt.
>
> 'Thirdly, that the Northern Irish Government has used Special

*Report of a Commission of Inquiry into the Special Powers Acts (NCCL, 1936; republished 1972). The members of the Commission were Edward Digby KC, JP; Margery Fry, former secretary to the Howard League for Penal Reform; William McKeag, a former Liberal MP and solicitor; Edward Mallalieu MA, a barrister and former Liberal MP. Its secretary was Neil Lawson, now Mr Justice Lawson.

Powers towards securing the domination of one particular political faction and, at the same time, towards curtailing the lawful activities of its opponents. The driving of legitmate movements underground into illegality, the intimidating or branding as law-breakers of their adherents, however innocent of crime, has tended to encourage violence and bigotry on the part of the Government's supporters as well as to beget in its opponents an intolerance of the 'law and order' thus maintained. The Government's policy is thus driving its opponents into the ways of extremists.'

The experience of the last 45 years and, particularly, of the last decade has borne out our contention that emergency powers are *not* a necessary and acceptable response to political violence, but one of the chief causes of continued violence. Denial of civil rights and the implementation of emergency powers feeds the conflict from which the terrorist emerges.

The Prevention of Terrorism Acts of 1974 and 1976 brought to Great Britain the emergency legislation under which Northern Ireland has been governed for over 50 years. The Acts have destroyed safeguards for the liberty of the individual won over centuries; by replacing legally defined and protected rights with arbitrary executive powers, they have violated cardinal principles of the rule of law.

These are strong condemnations. But they are justified by the examination of the extraordinary powers conferred on Ministers by the Acts. Central to the Acts is the power to *exclude* a United Kingdom citizen from Great Britain to Northern Ireland. The excluded person is not charged with a criminal offence. He can be detained over three weeks, with no right to *habeas corpus*. He has no right to a hearing or to appear before a court, and no right to an appeal. The United Kingdom Government is entirely blind to injustices which it roundly condemns when perpetrated by foreign dictatorships.

The NCCL is the only organisation which has monitored in detail the operation of the 1974 and 1976 Prevention of Terrorism Acts. We hope that, by bringing together information which is not available easily elsewhere, we will alert all those concerned with civil liberties — and in particular, Members of Parliament of all parties — to the dangers inherent in the continued existence of this law.

Patricia Hewitt
General Secretary, National Council for Civil Liberties
April 1981

Introduction

On 21 November 1974, 21 people died following two bomb explosions in Birmingham pubs. Although the alleged perpetrators were apprehended the same day and later convicted, a week of public outcry followed, which included demands for a ban on the IRA, for hanging of convicted terrorists and a new police campaign against the IRA, as well as violent attacks on some Irish people. On 28 November the then Home Secretary, Roy Jenkins, introduced the Prevention of Terrorism (Temporary Provisions) Bill. It was approved by Parliament without a division and came into force the next day.

The Act introduced to Great Britain the emergency legislation (first the Special Powers Acts 1922 and then the Emergency Provisions Act 1973) which had governed Northern Ireland for over 50 years. As other reports have shown, the use of repressive legislation has exacerbated the violence in Northern Ireland which then spread to the mainland — followed by the emergency legislation which helped create it.

The Prevention of Terrorism Act was based partly on the Emergency Provisions Act itself, as well as on the Prevention of Violence (Temporary Provisions) Act 1939, introduced in Great Britain in response to an earlier IRA campaign. But it is clear that the details of the 1974 Act had been secretly decided, long before its acceptance by Parliament. Just over 18 months previously — in the aftermath of the Old Bailey bombings of March 1973 — the Home Office, under a Conservative administration, had circulated what were described as 'contingency plans for dealing with terrorism in England'. Several draft Bills were drawn up to proscribe the IRA and to restrict the movement of Irish people from Eire into the UK; in the summer of 1974, the idea of exclusion orders was added to the list of proposals being considered by Government departments.

There were three sections to the Act, the first dealing with the banning of organisations; the second with the exclusion of suspected terrorists at the discretion of the Secretary of State; and the third with the extension of police powers to hold for questioning any person suspected of connection with terrorism. The measures were to last for six months only, although the Act could be renewed — in whole or in part — after that date.

The 1974 Act

From November 1974 to April 1975, NCCL carefully monitored the operation of the Act and published a report which was quoted extensively by MPs during the renewal debate in May 1975. Despite a sharp decline in bombing incidents, in that debate Roy Jenkins recommended a further six-month extension so that the law enforcement agencies would not be left powerless should the bombing campaign resume. But he emphasised the temporary nature of the Act and committed himself to ending it. On 19 May 1975 he said:

> 'I am prepared to tell the House that unless in November I feel able to recommend the dropping of substantial parts of the Act, I shall not ask the House to proceed by order.'

Yet on 28 November 1975 he asked the Commons to do exactly that — while a new Bill published a week previously could pass through its Parliamentary stages.

The new Bill, the basis of the present Act, amended the 1974 Act in three ways. It extended the period within which a person served with an exclusion order could make representations to the Home Office from 48 hours to 96 hours; gave such a person the right to a 'personal interview' with a government nominee; and doubled the lifespan of the Act to one year, after which it could be renewed for up to 12 months an indefinite number of times.

During the three Committee sittings on the Bill (totalling about eight hours discussion) the Conservative MPs and Enoch Powell MP (Official Unionist Party) were particularly vociferous, and amendments which stiffened and extended the Bill were later incorporated with Government agreement. Demands for compulsory identity cards and the reintroduction of hanging were, however, resisted.

The important changes later ratified by the Commons made it an offence not to pass on to the police information about terrorism, widened the provisions relating to financial and political support for proscribed organisations and provided for exclusion from Northern Ireland back to Great Britain. Amendments tabled on the floor of the Commons to abolish exclusion orders and to give the Judges' Rules statutory force were thrown out. The Act as amended became law on 25 March 1976.

The 1976 Act

With minor amendments, this Act has remained in force ever since.

In December 1977 an inquiry headed by Lord Shackleton was established to report on the operation of the Act. Its terms of reference were as follows:

> *Accepting the continuing need for legislation against terrorism*, to assess the operation of the Prevention of Terrorism (Temporary Provisions) Acts 1974 and 1976, with particular reference to the effectiveness of this legislation and its effects on the liberties of the subject. (our italics)

Thus, the enquiry excluded consideration of the need for 'emergency' legislation of this type. His recommendations, published in August 1978, can be summarised as follows:

— statistics on the operation of the Act should be published quarterly;
— exclusion order cases should be reviewed with the possibility of the orders being revoked;
— the government should reconsider its policy on financial assistance to relatives of excluded persons;
— section 11 (witholding information) should be allowed to lapse;
— improvements should be made in the diet and comfort of detainees;
— the Judges' Rules should be uniformly followed;
— fullest possible records of interviews should be kept;
— detention at ports should be for the same maximum period as elsewhere, i.e. seven days, not 12.

On 18 June 1979, the Home Secretary announced that exclusion orders would be reviewed after three years if the excluded person so wished. Those who were eligible and whose addresses were known to the Home Office were then approached. Since that date, detailed quarterly statistics on the operation of the Act have been produced by both the Home Office and the Northern Ireland Office.

On police advice, the Government has subsequently refused to allow section 11 to lapse and have turned down Lord Shackleton's suggestion that financial assistance be given to relatives on the grounds that 'such a scheme could not be justified' (statement by the Home Secretary, 1980).

The Prevention of Terrorism (Supplemental Temporary Provisions) Amendment Order 1979 was also agreed on 21 March 1979. From 18 April 1979 the length of time the police may detain a person at a port or airport on their own authority was reduced to 48 hours in line with their powers of detention elsewhere, the authority of the Secretary of State being required for an extension for a further five days.

On 3 July 1979, the Irish National Liberation Army was added to the schedule of proscribed organisations following their claim of responsibility for the assassination of a leading Conservative MP, Airey Neave.

The only other amendment involved a procedural change. In the renewal debate of 4 March 1980, the Home Secretary, stated that a new direction, to come into force on 25 March 1980, would enable an excluded person to be held for a further 24 hours beyond the seven days in police custody if arrangements were being made for his removal within that time. This, he said, was designed to prevent an excluded person from being transferred to prison from a police cell unnecessarily.

NCCL's objections to the Act

The Government originally justifed this 'draconian' Act, described by the Home Secretary as 'unprecedented in peacetime', on the grounds that a panic-stricken country would take the law into its own hands unless the Government stepped in. It was sold to a willing Parliament as a temporary expedient — an Act with built-in obsolescence which would automatically lapse unless emergency conditions justified renewal. The emergency nature of the legislation has now been largely forgotten — not least by the police — and the failure of a concerted campaign to repeal the Act has meant that it has, in practice, become an integral part of our criminal law.

Six years experience of the operation of the Acts have more than justified NCCL's initial opposition. The basic objections to the powers given to the Home Secretary and the police — the executive arm of government — may be summarised as follows.

In the United Kingdom, where the rights of citizens are not protected by a Bill of Rights, Parliamentary scrutiny and judicial review provide the only methods of preserving civil liberties in an emergency. But the 1974 Bill was rushed through all its Parliamentary stages in two days without any pretence of full and thorough scrutiny of its provisions. The 1976 Act doubled the period of renewal from six to 12 months, and renewal debates on both Acts have generally been brief and ill-attended. Although a small minority of MPs have stood out against the Acts, renewal has year after year secured the support of the overwhelming majority.

By giving the Home Secretary and the police powers which cannot be challenged in the courts, the Prevention of Terrorism Acts have destroyed at a stroke the edifice of safeguards built up in this country's legal system to protect the citizen against wrongful arrest, detention or conviction. Exclusion is identical in many essential respects to the discredited power to intern without trial: it allows the police, where they have no evidence on which to prosecute, to apply for an *executive* order against the suspect. The Home Secretary is given the unlimited power to decide — in secret and on the basis of evidence never made known to the suspect, his lawyers or the public — whether or not the suspect is in fact involved in terrorism. Thus, vital features of the rule of law — the right to know the charges, the right to hear and challenge the evidence, the right to a fair hearing and the right of appeal — are abolished. The open decision of a court has been replaced by the secret decision of the police, civil servants and a Minister. The inevitable result is that innocent people are deprived of their freedom on evidence which would never stand up to the scrutiny of a court of law.

Such administrative decisions will not reduce terrorism and may — by exacerbating hostility towards police and government — increase it. As NCCL stated in its evidence to the Royal Commission on Criminal Procedure:

> Arbitrary arrest has together with the power of search of the person contributed to a significant extent to the breakdown of the relationship between the police and many sections of the community. Every time a constable unjustifiably arrests a person, his action makes it harder for policing to be done effectively by increasing hostility to the police.

The NCCL predicted in 1974 that the existence of the new police powers combined with public pressure against Irish Republican sympathisers would lead the police to indulge in 'fishing trips' which would waste police manpower, result in few criminal convictions and harden attitudes. And the *Daily Mail* stated:

> The net effect of these special powers as far as the police are concerned is that they will be freer to harry, harass and interrogate terrorist suspects and terrorists sympathisers.

Now after each incident, such as the murder of Airey Neave or Lord Mountbatten, mass arrests under the Prevention of Terrorism Act are made and widely reported, although many of those detained are in fact not connected or involved with the crime which served as the pretext for their detention. The ordinary criminal law, which requires the suspect to be arrested on reasonable suspicion of an offence, gives the police more than adequate powers to bring suspects against whom there is real evidence to court: the Prevention of Terrorism Act, on the other hand, allows the police to arrest, detain and interrogate those against whom there is no evidence at all.

Central to the English legal system is the principle that a person is innocent until proved guilty. But repeatedly under this Act it is the innocent person who must establish his case. Those who have been detained and *released without charge* — the vast majority of those held under the Act — are frequently referred to by Home Secretaries as 'terrorists', while the records held on them by the police ensure that having once been detained and released they will again become objects of entirely unjustifiable suspicion. Someone faced with an exclusion order is offered the almost impossible task of persuading the Home Secretary and his advisers that the accusations against him — of which he knows nothing — are unfounded. The attitude amongst supporters of the Acts seems to be that this shift in the burden of proof is unimportant — after all, 'innocent people have nothing to fear'. The reality is that for 'innocent' one should read 'non-Irish, not involved or interested in Irish politics, does not live, work or mix socially with Irish people, does not read literature concerning Ireland, does not belong to a political party or other body which might be critical of British Government policy in Ireland'.

The experience of emergency powers in Northern Ireland has demonstrated that mass searches, arrests for interrogation, detentions to obtain confessions and internment without trial have been counterproductive in combating violence. The effect has been to harden attitudes amongst both communities. Civil liberty groups in Northern Ireland have recorded the increased reluctance of both Protestant and Catholic working-class communities to co-operate with the police and security forces following publicised instances of discriminatory or arbitrary action. In ending the use of the internment power, the Government itself acknowledged that executive powers which further undermined confidence in the institutions of the law could actually contribute to the violence with which they were designed to deal. Terrorist organisations must recruit to survive: recruitment is more easily sustained in a community resentful of the law and its operation. If the Prevention of Terrorism Act were used for the detention and exclusion of Irish people living in Britain on a larger scale — and there is nothing whatsoever in the Act to prevent mass arrests and expulsions — the result could well be a renewed spiralling of violence. The injustices which the operation of the Acts have so far caused in their use against the Irish community in Britain have already led to fear and alienation amongst ordinary, law-abiding families.

A further danger of 'emergency' powers is that they become permanent. The 1922 Special Powers Acts remained in force until replaced by the Emergency Provisions Act in 1973. The 1939 Prevention of Violence (Temporary Provisions) Act stayed on the statute books for 15 years. Campaigns to abolish the right to silence or reduce the right to jury trial in ordinary criminal cases are significantly strengthened when the police are given extraordinarily wide powers for some cases. When the Prevention of Terrorism Bill was first introduced, the police were reported to have urged longer detention powers as a special measure for 'terrorist' offences only, rejecting NCCL's contention that the Act's detention provisions in fact legitimised past police malpractice. By 1978, however, Metropolitan Police Commissioner Sir David McNee could openly admit — without significant public criticism — that suspects were frequently held for days on end. In his evidence to the Royal Commission on Criminal Procedure, Sir David asked for extended police powers which recognised the 'reality of interrogation methods', suggesting that in *all* cases the police should have a power to detain suspects for an initial 72 hours (the period provided for by the Emergency Provisions Act) followed by further, unlimited renewals of 72 hours each on the say-so only of a magistrate. Although the Royal Commission firmly rejected Sir David's suggestions, they proposed that for 'grave' offences, an initial period of 24 hours detention could be followed by an unlimited number of further 24-hour periods authorised by a magistrate sitting in private. (Unlike Sir David, they did propose that the suspect be legally represented at the magistrate's hearing.)

The European Convention on Human Rights permits governments to 'derogate' from most of its provisions during an emergency. Although the British Government has entered a notice of derogation for the Emergency Provisions Act, it has taken the view that the Prevention of Terrorism Act does not infringe the Convention. NCCL has challenged this view by representing a number of people arrested or excluded under the Act in cases under the Convention. In our view, the Act infringes Article 5 (the right to liberty), Article 6 (the right to a fair hearing), Article 8 (respect for private and family life), Articles 10 and 11 (freedom of expression and assembly) and Article 14 (prohibiting discrimination in the protection of these rights on grounds of national origin). Three cases of people detained under the Act have now been declared admissible by the Human Rights Commission.

Supporters of the Act argue that civil liberties must be sacrificed to deal with those suspected of terrorism. They are wrong. First, there is no evidence at all that the Act has been used to deal with terrorists: the vast majority of those arrested have been released without being charged or excluded. Secondly, the right to a fair trial is just as important for someone suspected of a terrorist crime as for any other suspect. Indeed, given the overwhelming horror which juries and judges rightly feel when dealing with terrorist crimes, safeguards for the suspect are arguably even more important than in lesser cases. But the abolition of all safeguards — indeed, the virtual replacement of trials in a court of law by secret executive decisions — immeasurably increases the risk that an *innocent* person will be convicted or excluded. The result is not only an injustice to the innocent person and his family: the result is that the genuinely guilty escape. Neither injustice nor inefficiency assists in the fight against crime. And thirdly, the Act's powers are unnecessary. The small minority of those arrested under the Act and later charged with a criminal offence could, and should, have been arrested under normal, pre-existing police powers, and brought before a court in the usual way.

Banned organisations

What the Act says

The Prevention of Terrorism Act gives the Secretary of State the power to ban an organisation which 'appears' to him to be concerned with terrorism in any part of the United Kingdom, relating to Northern Irish affairs. The Irish Republican Army was the only banned organisation specified in the 1974 Act and it has remained banned ever since. On 3 July 1979, the Irish National Liberation Army — which had claimed responsibility for the murder of Airey Neave — was also banned. No other organisations are banned under the Act.

'Terrorism' is defined as the use of violence for political ends and includes any use of violence for the purpose of putting the public or any section of the public in fear.

A person may not:

(i) belong to a proscribed organisation;
(ii) raise or receive money or goods on behalf of a proscribed organisation;
(iii) encourage any other form of support for a proscribed organisation;
(iv) organise a public or private meeting of more than two people in support of a proscribed organisation;
(v) organise a public or private meeting addressed by a member of a proscribed organisation, even if he is addressing the meeting on something unconnected with Northern Ireland affairs.

Maximum penalties are on conviction in a magistrates' court, a fine of £1000 and/or six months imprisonment, or if the case is heard in a Crown Court, an unlimited fine and/or five years imprisonment. The court may also forfeit any money and goods held for a proscribed organisation.

A person is not guilty of membership of a proscribed organisation if all his activities in it took place before it was proscribed. But it is up the defendant to prove this.

It is an offence to display, carry or wear in public anything which arouses a reasonable apprehension that you are a member or supporter of a proscribed organisation — even if you are not. Maximum penalties for this are a fine of £400 and/or six months imprisonment; these cases may only be heard in the magistrates' court.

In addition to these offences the 1976 Act also created a number of offences which relate to support for 'terrorism' in general, rather than to support for a proscribed organisation. Someone who knows or suspects that his money or goods are being used in connection with the 'commission, preparation or instigation' of acts of terrorism in the UK, connected with Northern Irish affairs, can be charged with an offence regardless of whether he is connected with a banned organisation.

It is an offence to:

(i) ask for a gift or loan which is intended to be used in connection with terrorism;
(ii) receive or accept any money or other goods which is intended to be used in this connection;
(iii) give or lend, or make available in any other way, any money or goods, knowing or suspecting it will be used in this connection. (Section 10.)

The penalties are the same as for the offences relating to banned organisations.

For any of these offences, as well as for those relating to banned organisations, a suspect can be arrested and detained without a warrant.

In 1976, when the new Bill was introduced, the Home Secretary was unperturbed by the fact that the section concerning banned organisations had hardly been used — producing one conviction in 16 months. He argued that it was preventive in intention, the absence of convictions being a sign of success! Despite this accomplishment, the Government proposed an increase in the penalties for openly displaying support for a proscribed organisation, from a £200 fine and/or three months' imprisonment to a £400 fine (later increased to £1000) and/or six months' imprisonment. No justification for the increased penalty was ever offered.

Section 10, relating to support for terrorism generally, was however a new departure. No loyalist paramilitary organisation has been banned under the Prevention of Terrorism Act. But support for a *lawful* organisation is now suspect.

In its report on offences against the person, published in March 1980, the Criminal Law Revision Committee rejected the proposal to make terrorism as such a criminal offence. It is easy to see why the Committee was right. 'Terrorism' is incapable of a precise definition, as the Prevention of Terrorism Act itself illustrates. Terrorist *activities* are already in themselves criminal offences. If terrorism itself is not an offence, it is wrong to make support for terrorism — falling short of involvement in terrorist activities — a crime. Any support for criminal activity, whether involving terrorists or anyone else, should be prosecuted under the general law of incitement, conspiracy or the liability of accomplices. Of the 49 people who have been prosecuted under the 1976 Prevention of Terrorism Act as a whole, 26 (53 per cent) have been convicted under section 10 — an indication that the section is used where there is no evidence of support for, or involvement in, a banned organisation and no evidence of criminal activities.

The record

Only one person was charged and convicted for support of a proscribed organisation under the 1974 Act. He was James Fegan, of Glasgow, convicted in February 1975 of soliciting support for the IRA by offering posters for sale. He had allegedly been heard in a bar asking drinkers whether they wanted to buy a poster to 'support the boys'. He had not sold any of the posters. He was sentenced to six months' imprisonment. Two others — Gerald McMorrow and William McGuigan — charged at the same time as Fegan were acquitted.

Under the 1976 Act, 42 people had been prosecuted in Great Britain by 30 June 1980. Of the 34 who were initially arrested under the Act, three have been charged with soliciting or receiving money for a proscribed organisation, of whom only one has been convicted. The bulk of convictions have been under Section 10. Three convictions were for soliciting money for use on acts of terrorism; 18 convictions were for receiving money or property for such use. One person was acquitted of receiving goods and charges were dropped in one further case. Two people were charged with both offences, of whom one was acquitted and one convicted. Finally there were two successful prosecutions for soliciting and giving money for use in acts of terrorism, and a further two for giving money or property for such use. In addition eight people were charged with receiving money or property without first having been detained under the Act. In four cases, charges were not proceeded with; the remaining four were found guilty and sentenced to five years imprisonment.

Of those convicted, fifteen were imprisoned for over five years; eleven for between one and five years; and two for one year or under. None were fined. These figures related to Great Britain only as at 30 June 1980.

In August 1980, two members of the Revolutionary Communist Group were arrested for selling papers allegedly in support of the Provisional IRA and were charged with displaying items in public which could give rise to an apprehension that they were members of a proscribed organisation. The charge was later replaced by a charge of soliciting financial support for a proscribed organisation and the defendants were remanded *in custody* for a week. At the trial, however, the Prevention of Terrorism Act charge was dropped completely — and replaced by breach of the peace!

The effect of bans

Proscription has inevitably led to the curtailing of debate and legitimate political activity by groups campaigning peacefully on Irish matters. The passing of the Act created an unease — in part justified — that a person could be charged for beliefs rather than criminal activity. The form of words used blurs the distinction between members of a banned organisation and Republican or Loyalist sympathisers. After November 1974 both Provisional Sinn Fein and Clann na h'Eireann, which pursue political campaigns for similar objectives to those of the Provisional and Official IRA respectively, restricted their political activity for fear of a charge under the Act. The atmosphere at that time can be gauged from press reports that people were afraid to be associated with anything Irish. Even Irish harps had apparently been destroyed!

NCCL has been consulted by many different groups on issues which range from selling of Easter Lilies (which commemorate the Rising of 1916 in Dublin) to raising money for prisoners' families and selling newspapers. It certainly appeared that the selling of Republican papers was an invitation for an arrest and interrogation under the Act by the police. During 1979, for instance, five supporters of 'Hands Off Ireland' (a campaign organised by the Revolutionary Communist Group) were arrested.

Press, radio and television have become increasingly reluctant to promote views hostile to government policy on Ireland. In June 1980, the British Film Institute presented a double bill of two films originally shot for HTV and ATV, 'Curious Journey' and 'Hang Out Your Brightest Colours', but suppressed by the television companies on grounds of 'lack of balance'. Both films were highly critical of British presence in Ireland. The films were only shown at all because one was returned to the narrator for £1 and the other was obtained by the BFI in its capacity as national film archivists.

NCCL has also been told of local groups' reluctance to show films such as 'Ireland Behind the Wire' which were critical of the treatment of the minority community in Northern Ireland in general, and of internment and its implementation by the British Army in particular. NCCL also received reports that many pubs and clubs had refused access to collectors of any description, even from charities with established credentials.

Certainly since 1974 there has been an increasing reluctance on the part of those with no direct commitment to Northern Ireland politics to involve themselves in any way, however peripheral. The Troops Out Movement have on numerous occasions experienced difficulties in booking halls. Rallies are banned from Trafalgar Square if they relate to Northern Ireland or are called by an organisation connected with the province (the Peace People were given special dispensation by the Secretary of State for Environment). Even the British Peace Committee were refused permission to hold a rally in the square.

The Act also affects in a fundamentally racist way the lives of Irish people in Britain. Tom Walsh, public relations officer and former chairman of the Federation of Irish Societies in Britain has written to NCCL as follows:

> The Prevention of Terrorism Act affects the ordinary Irish person living and working in this country . . . The only qualification to be suspect and to be questioned, fingerprinted, photographed (by the police) is to be Irish. The only way the tragic circumstances of the last ten years can be brought to a happy conclusion is for there to be discussions and political debate and constant seeking for a solution but this possibility is hindered by the PTA. Irish people, since the Act became law, are afraid to discuss the situation, are afraid to be in possession of or read articles and literature about the situation . . .
>
> The Act has been tragically successful in that it has terrified the ordinary Irish people in this country. I have met people who are afraid to write to their MP or to a newspaper expressing concern about the situation in the North. I know people who threw away books on Ireland which were treasured possessions. I know people who want to object to the more obnoxious and insulting 'Irish jokes' but who are afraid to because they remember vaguely the publicity at the introduction of the Act and how easy it would be to be branded a terrorist.

It was clear at an early stage in the Act's operation that the bans themselves were not of major importance. Both the Home Office and the police had argued against a ban on the IRA until after the Birmingham bombings when the ban was said to be necessary to placate public opinion. The real value of the ban, in the eyes of the authorities, was that it allowed a wide range of activities unconnected with criminal offences to be curtailed. Ian Gilmour MP, who was spokesman for the Conservative Party during the 1974 debate on the Act, confirmed his party's view when he said in that debate: 'I think, too, that it has cut down the activities of both the political wings of both the Provisional and Official IRA, and that also is to the good.' The same party has (rightly in NCCL's view) rejected calls for a ban on the National Front or its political activities on the grounds that, however objectionable their views, democracy demands that they be allowed to exist.

Against the bans

Membership of an illegal organisation is difficult to prove, unless admitted. In Northern Ireland the frequent refusal of members of paramilitary organisations to recognise the court is usually taken as an admission of guilt. Most of those charged with 'membership' in Northern Ireland were also charged with a more serious offence, so that if the judge acquitted the defendant of the heavier offence, the membership charge acted as a net to ensure conviction.

Proscription has been rejected in the past on the basis that the police considered it would make detection more difficult. Roy Jenkins made it clear, when introducing the ban, that proscription itself would not reduce terrorism. Previous Home Secretaries had refused to consider proscription on the grounds that new organisations with the same aims and methods would emerge under a different name or that activities and supporters would disappear underground, hampering the surveillance work of the police. On this point, however, it should be noted that there is nothing to prevent the Secretary of State banning the IRA and 'like organisations', so that groups may be banned without their knowledge.

Lord Shackleton in his report stated that proscription of the IRA had not, in the view of the police, made more than a marginal contribution to the curtailment of the activities of the IRA, and the justification for it did not derive principally from its 'operational' value.

The only argument which supporters of proscription can muster is that public opinion would be affronted if this part of the Act were allowed to lapse.

By its nature, proscription is arbitrary. The 1976 Act allows the Secretary of State to ban an organisation 'if it appears' to him to be involved in terrorism connected with Northern Irish affairs. There is no enquiry. Evidence need not be produced. No appeal is permitted by the organisation banned. There is no Parliamentary debate. The choice of the word 'appears' is designed deliberately to exclude judicial review. The Minister's decision can only be challenged if it can be *proved* that he acted in bad faith, an impossible burden to discharge.

The full potential of the power to ban has been recognised by the police. In a recent pamphlet published by Police Review Publications, entitled *Public Order and the Police*, the following appeared:

> A much simpler action to prevent any of our present troubles would be to declare the National Front, the Socialist Workers' Party or whatever party is causing trouble to be a proscribed organisation under the Prevention of Terrorism (Temporary Provisions) Act 1976.

The pamphlet was written by Kenneth Sloan, training officer with the Manchester Police, and carried an introduction by William Whitelaw, now Home Secretary.

As Martin Flannery MP said in the 1980 renewal debate: 'There is a spirit of witch hunt and retribution calling for the proscription of groups that have nothing proven against them under the Act.'

There is no doubt that many people in Northern Ireland, as in Great Britain, find the views of Republican supporters offensive — just as many people find the views of Loyalists and Orange Order members offensive. The Act has not prevented the publication and distribution in Northern Ireland of Republican newspapers which describe the Provisional IRA as freedom fighters and attacks on civilians and soldiers as victories. Nor has it prevented the expression of extreme Orange views. The literature whose distribution had led to prosecutions under the Act in Great Britain is in fact far less 'offensive' than much which is freely obtained in Northern Ireland. The effect of the Act is simply to restrict even further the range of opinions available to those people in Britain interested in the situation in Northern Ireland.

But the central point is that no organisation should be banned and no publication censored simply because it is offensive. Freedom of association and expression, which are fundamental to political activity in a democracy, involve the right to make one's views known and to organise with others of a similar conviction. It is inevitable that some views expressed in a democratic community will be deeply objectionable to other people. They will also be deeply objectionable to those in authority, who are inevitably tempted to respond, not to the arguments or views expressed, but by banning the organisation or prosecuting the individuals involved.

Moreover, a brief examination of the history of Northern Ireland shows just how futile bans are. The ban on the IRA and other organisations under the Emergency Provisions Act has not prevented the organisations from existing. Nor has the ban diminished support for their views. The various means used by the British Goverment within Great Britain itself to curtail the expression of different points of view about Northern Ireland have simply helped to ensure that the British public has little or no understanding of the situation in that part of the country and that the Government can take almost any measures without serious debate or opposition. That policy of censorship has not helped the British Government achieve security or peace in Northern Ireland; it has seriously undermined democratic freedoms throughout the whole of the United Kingdom; and it has left the public, most MPs and most of the press utterly complacent about the measures which it is right for a government to take in dealing with opposition.

Exclusion orders

What the Act says

Under this part of the Act, it is important to remember that Great Britain means England, Scotland and Wales; United Kingdom means Great Britain and Northern Ireland.

Under the Act, any Secretary of State — it will usually be the Home Secretary or Northern Ireland Secretary — can decide to make an exclusion order against a person if:

(i) it appears to him expedient, in order to prevent acts of terrorism intended to influence Goverment policy or public opinion with respect to Northern Ireland affairs, *and*
(ii) he believes that a person is or has been concerned in the 'commission, preparation or instigation, of acts of terrorism, *or*
(iii) he believes that a person is attempting to enter Great Britain or Northern Ireland, with a view to being concerned in the 'commission, preparation or instigation of acts of terrorism.

'Terrorism' is defined as the use of violence for political ends and includes any use of violence for the purpose of putting the public or any section of the public in fear. The definition is wide enough to include almost any connection, however remote, with terrorist activity.

UK Citizens

If a person is a United Kingdom citizen he cannot be excluded from the United Kingdom completely. But he can be restricted to living either in Northern Ireland or in Great Britain.

He can be excluded from Great Britain to Northern Ireland:

(i) unless he has ordinarily been resident in Great Britain for the last 20 years (not including time spent in prison in the United Kingdom, Channel Isles or Isle of Man); *or*
(ii) unless he was born in Great Britain and has been ordinarily resident there all his life; *or*
(iii) unless he has already been excluded from Northern Ireland.

He can be excluded from Northern Ireland to Great Britain:

(i) unless he has ordinarily been resident in Northern Ireland; *or*
(ii) unless he has already been excluded from Great Britain.
If a person objects to an exclusion order on any of these grounds, it is up to him to prove his case.

Citizens of other countries

A citizen of a foreign country can be excluded from the United Kingdom altogether and can be sent to the country he is most closely connected with.

Effects of an Exclusion Order

A United Kingdom citizen subject to an exclusion order is removed from Great Britain to Northern Ireland and is prohibited from entering Great Britain or being there. The Act permits someone to be excluded *from* Northern Ireland to Britain, but no such exclusion orders have been made. No UK citizen can be excluded from both Northern Ireland and Great Britain.

A citizen of a foreign country who is excluded will be prohibited from entering or being in any part of the United Kingdom.

The excluded person can make representations against exclusion within 96 hours of notice being served upon him and he also has a right to request an oral hearing before a government Adviser. In 1980, the Advisers were Lord Alport, Lord Underhill and John Newey QC.

If the Secretary of State does not consider the representations frivolous, he will refer them to the Adviser. If a request for an interview with the Adviser is made and the person has not 'voluntarily' left the country, he has a right to such an interview. If he has been removed with his 'consent' but changes his mind within the 96 hour limit, he may make written representations but has no right to an oral hearing. If a person is served with an exclusion order, he is normally transferred from police custody to prison seven days after arrest. From 25 March 1980, a person may be held in police custody for a further 24 hours (eight days in all) if arrangements are being made for his removal — that it, either he consents to removal or has made no representations. After receiving the representations and, where applicable, the report of the Adviser, the Secretary of State will make his own decision as to whether or not the order should be revoked.

A person subject to an exclusion order has no right:

— to know the evidence on which the exclusion order is made;

— to cross-examine on the evidence;
— to have a public or formal hearing;
— to know on what basis the representations were successful or unsuccessful;
— to appeal to a court or tribunal against exclusion.

The Secretary of State may at any time revoke an exclusion order by a further order. Following the Shackleton Report, the Home Secretary announced on 18 June 1979 that each exclusion order would be reviewed three years after it was made.

Criminal offences

Under the Act, it is a criminal offence:

(i) not to obey an exclusion order once notice has been served;
(ii) to help any person who is known or ought to be known to be subject to an exclusion order, to enter the country against the order;
(iii) to harbour a person who is subject to an exclusion order.

For any of these offences a person may be arrested without a warrant although the Attorney General must give his consent before prosecution. Maximum penalty on conviction in the magistrates' court is £1000 fine and/or six months' imprisonment; in the Crown Court an unlimited fine and/or five years' imprisonment.

Detention at ports of entry

Under the Act, if a person is entering or leaving Great Britain or Northern Ireland (including people coming in as transit passengers), he can be detained at the port of entry, while the Secretary of State decides if he wants to make an exclusion order. The person can be detained by any 'examining officer' — i.e. a police officer, an immigration officer or a customs officer working as an immigration officer (and, in the case of Northern Ireland only, a soldier). The Government has given an undertaking that a person subject to an exclusion order, in transit at a United Kingdom port, will not be deemed to have broken his exclusion order.

A person can be detained for 48 hours and then for another five days on the authority of the Secretary of State pending a decision whether or not to make an exclusion order.

The record in Great Britain

Between 29 November 1974 and 30 September 1980, 291 applications for an exclusion order were made, of which 35 were refused by the Home Secretary. Ten orders were revoked before the person was removed, and eleven others were revoked after the person had been removed. Of these 21 revocations, 13 were revoked following representations (out of a total of 41 contested orders); two following a review of 20 orders, which had been in force for three years; six 'for other reasons'. Of the 256 exclusion orders made, 171 were made against a person detained at a port or airport and 61 against a person detained elsewhere. Twenty-four were made against a person not detained under the Act. Two hundred and one excluded persons were returned to Northern Ireland, 34 to the Republic of Ireland. Ten persons were already outside Great Britain when the order was made. No-one was excluded from Northern Ireland to Great Britain.

The arguments for Exclusion Orders

The Government argues that its job is to prevent acts of terrorism as well as to ensure that criminals are punished. It is therefore necessary to anticipate events, and to take action even in circumstances where the available evidence would not secure a conviction. Court action would be preferable but, they argue, the type of evidence gathered by police against excluded people is 'too sensitive', relates to 'national security' or would not otherwise stand up in court. Lord Shackleton termed it 'highly classified'.

'Sensitive information' often comes from paid informers or other unnamed sources, who remain unidentified and cannot therefore be called to court as witnesses. National security would cover almost any matter relating to the strategy and tactics of the police in dealing with terrorist-type offences. According to the Shackleton report, the police prepare the case for exclusion at a special office in New Scotland Yard, staffed by Metropolitan and provincial Special Branch members. If approved by a commander, the application is forwarded to the Home Office, where it is considered by various officials, the Minister, and finally the Secretary of State who must sign it.

The arguments against

The introduction of exclusion orders has given the United Kingdom its own system of 'internal exile'.

Lord Shackleton concluded: 'Exclusion is not a judicial proceeding and it involves no charges, trial or court. Nor is it a punishment'. But exclusion involves compulsory removal to another part of the country; separation from friends and, often, family; a prohibition on return; and, for those returned to Northern Ireland, a risk of injury or death in the violence. It is precisely because exclusion is a punishment imposed *without* judicial proceedings that it is so objectionable.

The majority of exclusion orders have been made against United Kingom citizens who are now forced to live in Northern Ireland, even though they have chosen to live in Britain and have been resident here for anything up to 20 years. An excluded person has no right to know what he is suspected of, no right to hear or challenge the evidence, no right to a trial. Because the police 'evidence' against him is known only to government ministers, civil servants and the Adviser, any independent assessment of its worth is impossible.

Lord Shackleton himself admitted that the value of the information in the police dossier depended on 'careful gradings and assessment'. The dossier contains information such as any criminal record, information about political activity as well as unsubstantiated statements obtained by the police, possibly after a suspect has been detained for several days under the Act.

Uncorroborated statements may also be obtained from informers whose motives must be suspect. There may be financial pressure or personal malice involved. There is no way of testing whether an informer in fact acted as an *agent provocateur*, who actively encouraged the person to engage in illegal activity. Statements may be supplied by someone eager to satisfy the police or by someone with a personal grudge against the suspect or from people also held under the Act itself.

Silence during the interrogation may also encourage the police to apply for an exlusion order. Lord Shackleton stated in his report:

> The police often find that the person concerned will say nothing to them at all. They realise that there can be several reasons for this and indeed the person concerned is not bound to say anything. But the police cannot rule out the possibility that he has been trained in what might be called 'anti-interrogation' techniques and that this may be an indication of involvement in a terrorist organisation.

The police are certainly anxious to reduce the suspect's present right to remain silent. They support the continuation of section 11 of the Act (see below, page 54) which makes it an offence to withhold information from the police. In evidence to the Royal Commission on Criminal Procedure, the Metropolitan Police Commissioner, Sir David McNee, recommended that a refusal to answer questions should be taken into account at any subsequent court hearing, so that guilt could be inferred from silence. Such a proposal caused furious protest from the legal profession when it was made by the Criminal Law Revision Committee in 1972. The legal position — endorsed by the Royal Commission — remains that a suspect's silence may not be used against him in court. But the police have used the extraordinarily wide discretion given them by the Prevention of Terrorism Act to use silence as 'proof' of involvement in terrorism — and, therefore, as the basis for exclusion — even where there is no evidence of criminal activities.

As long as the suspect and his lawyer are refused the right to know the accusations made against him, the right to challenge the evidence and cross-examine prosecution witnesses, and the right to a judicial hearing and appeal, there must be an overwhelming probability that people are excluded on the basis of inaccurate evidence. But an exclusion order can be as damning as a criminal conviction.

Legal advice obtained by the NCCL indicates that it is *impossible* to challenge an exclusion order in the courts. The Act gives the Secretary of State the power to exclude anyone provided he is 'satisfied' that the excludee is involved in terrorism. The Home Secretary's subjective judgement can only be challenged if the excluded person can show evidence that the decision was made in bad faith — an impossible task. The only way of establishing evidence of bad faith would be to commence a legal action and obtain all the documentation involved in the case — but such disclosure would be refused on the grounds that it would be damaging to 'the public interest'.

Successive Home Secretaries have said or implied that those served with exclusion orders are dangerous criminals. In 1976, for instance, the then Home Secretary, Roy Jenkins, said that people appealing against an exclusion order could not be freed while the representations were dealt with. 'It will not be possible to say that someone is a grave security risk to this country and, in the circumstances we have experienced recently, allow them to go about their ordinary business while a decision is arrived at . . . what are here involved are the gravest matters of national security.'

The obvious inference that a bomb in Belfast is not as politically damaging as bomb in Birmingham was noted with anger by many, and particularly by the MPs from Northern Ireland. As a palliative, the 1976 Act allows a person to be excluded from Northern Ireland back to Great Britain although the Home Secretary admitted that this amendment was accepted in deference to Northern Irish sen-

sibilities, and not because he believed it would have any practical effect. It is easy to imagine the public fury which could be caused if the export of allegedly dangerous terrorists to Northern Ireland becomes a two-way trade.

NCCL believes that the system of exclusion violates the European Convention on Human Rights, Article 6 of which provides that in the determination of his civil rights or in any criminal proceedings against him, everyone is entitled to a fair and public hearing within a reasonable time by an independent and impartial tribunal established by law. Furthermore, anyone charged with an offence has the right to be informed of the nature and cause of the accusation against him and to challenge witnesses. Article 14 of the Convention provides that implementation of Convention rights must be made without discrimination on grounds of religion or national origin. And Article 13 provides that anyone who believes that his Convention rights have been infringed shall have the right to a remedy within his own country. As we have seen, it is impossible to challenge an exclusion order in the British courts, while *habeas corpus* has proved ineffective in Prevention of Terrorism Act cases (see page 45).

The existence of the exclusion power has made it impossible for the United Kingdom to ratify Protocol Four of the Convention, which declares the right to freedom of movement within one's own country and the right to choose one's own residence.

In October 1980, NCCL initiated a complaint to the European Human Rights Commission on behalf of **Danny Ryan**, who was born in Ireland. He was living with his family in Bristol when he was arrested under the Prevention of Terrorism Act in January 1975 and served with an exclusion order. His representations were unsuccessful and he was removed to Dublin. As a result, he has been separated from his five eldest children who have stayed in England, and his two younger children, who joined him in Dublin, were forced to interrupt their education, abandon their schools and leave the rest of their family. In July 1979, he applied to the Home Secretary for a review of the exclusion order which had by then been in force for over four years. The Home Secretary refused to revoke the order and Danny Ryan has complained to the European Commission of the continuing infringement of his right to family life. No decision on admissability has yet been made.

How Exclusion Orders work

Within an hour of the 1974 Act coming into operation, Scotland

Yard presented the Home Secretary with a file containing the names of alleged IRA activists whom it wanted excluded from the country. The first applications were all made by the Special Branch and were reportedly accompanied by documentary evidence indicating the involvement of those people named. The list of excluded persons was then issued to the press by the Home Office.

As the figures indicate, suspects have tended not to contest exclusions orders once notice has been served. Only 41 out of 279 had objected to the order by June 1980.

The notice of exclusion gives no reasons for the decision to exclude. In the case of a non-United Kingdom citizen excluded from the United Kingdom, the notice takes the following form:

> The Secretary of State is satisfied that you ______ are concerned in the commission, preparation or instigation of acts of terrorism. In pursuance of sections 4(1) and 6 of the Prevention of Terrorism (Temporary Provisions) Act 1976 the Secretary of State has made an exclusion order prohibiting you ______ from being in, or entering the United Kingdom. Under Section 9 of the Act a person against whom an exclusion order has been made commits an offence if he fails to comply with the order. The maximum penalty for this offence is five years imprisonment, and unlimited fine or both.
>
> If you object to the exclusion order you may, within 96 hours, make representations to the Secretary of State in writing setting out the grounds of your objection. You have a right to a personal interview with a person, appointed by the Secretary of State, who will advise him on your case. If you wish to make representations objecting to the making of the order and you wish to have a personal interview with the adviser, you should send your representations and request to the Secretary of State, Home Office, Whitehall, London SW1.
>
> I, ______ do/do not* wish to make representations objecting to the exclusion order which the Secretary of State had made against me. I do/do not* wish to have an interview with an adviser to the Secretary of State.
>
> (*delete where applicable).

A solictor is thus in the impossible position of hazarding guesses at the police evidence and attempting to refute unknown allegations in making representations to the Home Secretary. He is in no position to explore the evidence with his client or to pursue any line of enquiry not supplied by this client. Furthermore, he has no legal right to be present at the interview with the Adviser.

The existence of the Adviser is an attempt to disguise the unfettered nature of the power given to the Home Secretary and in no way represents an impartial assessment of the case.

Lord Alport, one of the two original Advisers, did not at first look at the police evidence before he interviewed the suspect. Indeed he made a virtue of this decision by saying he would not wish to ask awkward questions! The following is taken from the transcripts of an interview:

> 'My name is Alport. I am one of the advisers appointed by the Home Secretary to give him advice as to whether an exclusion order should be maintained or revoked. This is not a court of law. This is not an interrogation by me. The object is to try and add to the background of the grounds for the representations that you have made against the exclusion order, so that I may be able to judge fairly to the best of my ability as to what advice I give to the Secretary of State. I have not seen the police evidence. I have not done so for two reasons. One is that I wanted to meet you and ask you certain questions in order to get from you certain information which may be helpful to me in making my decision. I do not want to be prejudiced in any way at this particular moment at our interview by having read a record of whatever allegations are made against you by the police. That is the first reason.
>
> 'The second reason is that I do not want to be placed in a position whereby I might ask you questions which might be of an incriminating nature. Therefore I come to meet you on this occasion having before me only two documents'. (A letter from the excluded person and another from his solicitor).

It is particularly disturbing that the Advisers do not need any particular legal experience or any knowledge of Northern Ireland or of political groups operating in Britain. If the police evidence is not discussed, the interview can do no more than provide the Adviser with a general impression of the suspect's credibility. This may hinge on his involvement with perfectly legal political groups of which the Adviser may disapprove — he may for instance be more inclined to recommend exclusion for a supporter of a united Ireland than for a person advocating continuing direct rule. The standard of advice rests solely upon the Adviser, for he can adopt any procedure for the interview he thinks fit.

Aware of a police dossier of allegedly incriminating evidence (which the suspect has not seen and cannot rebut), the Adviser might be expected at the very least to inform himself of the political views of the potential excludee. What group does he belong to? Does it support military action? What is its attitude to the political use of violence? And so on. The following quotation is taken from a transcript of an interview which took place after four members of Clann na h'Eireann had already been excluded on Lord Alport's advice.

(The suspect has just said that he is a member of Sinn Fein in Britain).

Alport: This is completely different from Cann na h'Eirinn? *(sic)*.

Answer: Completely.

Alport: Is this the Provisional?

Answer: Yes, Sinn Fein.

Alport: The Provisional side of it?

Answer: This is right.

Alport: Cann na h'Eirinn *(sic)* is the political wing of the Official IRA, is that correct?

Answer: That is correct.

Alport: This is the political wing of the Provisional IRA?

Answer: Yes.

Excluded Persons

Former Home Secretary, Roy Jenkins, claims to have rid Britain of 'dangerous terrorists' — 'the most experienced leaders of the Official and Provisional IRA'. One would expect such people to be of considerable interest to the security forces of Northern Ireland, which has been landed with most of these 'experienced leaders'. But only one excluded person has been arrested and charged with an offence.

Of the 48 people excluded during 1979, one was a young man who had only just arrived in Britain — having come here with the help of the Royal Ulster Constabulary itself! **'John Smith'** had been arrested and convicted in Belfast, while a teenager, on charges of IRA membership and involvement in a hijack and arson. During his prison sentence, the Provisional IRA came to believe that he had given information to the security services. Knowing that his life would be in danger after he was released from prison, he sought the help of the Peace People who, with the RUC's assistance, arranged for him to come to Britain. He was released from prison in November 1979. It was accepted during the trial that he was, at most, a reluctant member of the Provisional IRA and his probation officer and the Peace People believed he was determined to get away from Belfast and start a new life. Shortly after his release from prison, he came to Britain and went to the home of the family which had agreed to put him up while he looked for a job. The following day, he was arrested by the police and held for seven days. He was served with an exclusion order and returned to Belfast. Representations made by his solicitor and probation officer were unsuccessful.

In February 1978, **John McKenna** was excluded. He had come to live in Britain five years earlier and married an English woman. They settled in Kent and had two children. He was arrested under the Act, detained from questioning, transferred to Brixton prison and served with an exclusion order. His representations were rejected and he was flown to Belfast. Like other excluded persons, he was not arrested there and he returned to the Falls, to the Catholic estate in Belfast where he had grown up. His English wife — who is not a Catholic — and their two daughers decided they had no choice but to follow him, even though his wife had little prospect of settling down and neither of them has any prospect of getting a job. The Kent solicitor who made representations on his behalf objected strongly to the whole proceeding:

> The Act however works extremely harshly and no doubt unfairly in cases such as Mr McKenna where there must be a real doubt as to whether or not he was really involved in any terrorist activities in Northern Ireland or in England which would have justified his exclusion from England . . . One of my main concerns with this case is the fact that Mr McKenna's wife is English and the two children of the marriage were born in England whereas the making of the exclusion order virtually forced her and the children to leave their country of origin.

The solicitor also pointed out, that since the suspect faced with an exclusion order is never charged with a criminal offence, no legal aid is available other than the extremely limited 'Green Form' scheme. The excludee therefore either has to find private funds or depend on the willingness of a solicitor to take on the case without payment.

On 12 December 1979, the police raided a large number of homes in London, Southampton, Birmingham and Liverpool. Amongst those detained in Southampton were **James Martin**, his wife and two of their children. A third child was away at the time. Although Veronica Martin and the children were released after 11 hours, James was detained for seven days until he was excluded. After reaching Northern Ireland, he made unsuccessful representations. James had lived in this country for 19 years — only one year short of the time-limit for exemption from exclusion. All three children were born in Britain. The Martin family decided they had no option but to go to Belfast.

Because of the exclusion order, James Martin lost his job and Veronica did not work. The Northern Ireland Housing Executive refused to house them and Veronica was unable to obtain financial assistance with the costs of removing their furniture from their council house in Southampton.

In many cases, the exclusion of the only or main breadwinner forces the family to choose between going to Belfast or remaining in poverty in Britain. The family may have left Belfast in the first place to escape the troubles; the wife and children may in fact be English and understandably unwilling to move to a strange city, devastated by a decade of violence. The problems are even greater if the marriage is 'mixed'. As Gerry Fitt MP said about a number of his constituents during the debate on the 1976 Bill:

> 'The men involved are Belfast men married to English wives, and their children are English born. The men have been in steady jobs while they have live in Southampton. Their children go to English schools and speak with English accents. They are unsuited to be sent back to Northern Ireland to live in areas where an English accent might get them into trouble. I have spoken to these people and I am convinced that they are not and never have been involved in terrorist activities in this island.'

If a wage-earner is imprisoned following conviction in the courts, the families are helped by the state with the cost of travel to the prisons. Exclusion denies them such help. Although Lord Shackleton suggested that families should be given finanical aid to help with visiting, the Home Secretary said in the March 1980 renewal debate: 'I have considered the possibility of providing assistance towards the removal expenses of such families, but I have come to the conclusion that such a scheme would not be justified.'

The power of exclusion does not affect only those against whom an order is made. NCCL has received disturbing reports from people who allege that, having travelled from Ireland or Northern Ireland to Britain, they have been ordered by the police to return home. With the threat of detention and permanent exclusion hanging over them, such people do not normally protest: but the 'exclusion' never appears in the offical record.

In October 1980, NCCL was contacted by a probation officer at Maidstone prison. One of her clients, who had been convicted of conspiracy to cause explosions, had been granted parole on the advice of the Parole Board. The day before he was due to be released, he was informed by the governor that he would be detained for a further 15 days while the Home Secretary decided whether or not to exclude him. The Parole Board must have taken into account the nature of this man's offence before deciding to recommend him for parole. They were impressd by the fact that he had a home and a job to return to, and presumably believed that he was not likely to become involved in crime again. It therefore seems extraordinary that the Home Secretary should overrule the Parole Board's decision in this fashion.

Exclusion orders revoked

Of the 41 people who had made representations against an exclusion order up to the end of September 1980, only 13 had their order revoked. Very few people challenge the order: not because they admit the guilt but because they are unwilling to remain in prison for several days or weeks awaiting a final decision or reluctant to submit themselves to the farcical procedures involved in making representations.

Following a recommendation of Lord Shackleton, the Home Secretary now reviews exclusion orders which have been in force for three years. If the excluded person's present address is known, he receives a letter inviting him to apply for a review. Otherwise, he is invited to write to the Police Department of the Home Office — a requirement hardly likely to encourage someone who wants no further attention from the police. The excluded person asking for a review is required to complete a form giving details of all home addresses and employers since exclusion. By the end of September 1980, 94 people became eligible for a review of their exclusion order, of whom only 26 asked for a review to be undertaken. The first 20 reviews were completed by the end of September — a mere two orders were revoked as a result.

Unlike a prison sentence, an exclusion order has no end. It remains in force until the Home Secretary and unless the Home Secretary decides to lift it — or until the exclusion order provisions are finally allowed to lapse.

Arrest and detention

What the Act says

Arrests

Under the Act, a police constable can arrest a person without a warrant if he reasonably suspects:

(i) that he belongs to or supports a proscribed organisation and/or
(ii) that he is subject to an exclusion order, or has helped or harboured any other person who is subject to an exclusion order and/or
(iii) that he is concerned in the 'commission, preparation or instigation of acts of terrorism' — whether or not these are concerned with Northern Ireland affairs.

Detention

Once a person has been arrested he can be held by the police for up to 48 hours and then for another five days on the authority of the Secretary of State. During this time a suspect need not be charged with an offence, nor brought to court. This is a massive departure from the normal legal position which, even for serious offences, requires the suspect to be brought before a court 'as soon as practicable' after being charged.

The Judges' Rules — the guidelines for treatment of people under police questioning — apply to arrests under the Act. So a suspect should be allowed to contact his family and a solicitor; remain silent when questioned; and to consult a solicitor. But Section 11, making it an offence to withhold information has effectively abolished the right of silence, and many of those detained under the Act are not allowed to see a lawyer or contact friends.

Section 62 of the Criminal Law Act 1977 also applies, entitling a person who has been arrested to have a person informed of his arrest and place of custody without unnecessary delay.

After the arrest the police are allowed to take any 'reasonably necessary steps' for identification, including photographing and fingerprinting. This can be done without the suspect's consent and without a court order. 'Reasonable force' can be used if the suspect does not co-operate. These powers, again, destroy the normal safeguards under which a suspect can only be fingerprinted with his consent or under a court order.

Search

The Act also gives the police the power to stop and search, without a warrant, anyone suspected of involvement in terrorism, in order to establish whether the suspect has any documents or articles on him which could show that he was also liable for arrest.

A police officer who is searching premises with a search warrant is allowed under the Act to search every person found in the premises named in the warrant. An officer with the rank of superintendent or above can sign a note authorising a search, if he considers the case is one of great emergency and immediate action is necessary 'in the interest of the state' — thus removing the need to obtain a magistrate's approval.

Any officer using these powers of search, can seize anything which he has reasonable grounds for suspecting to be evidence of an offence relating to a proscribed organisation or an exclusion order. He can also take anything which he reasonably suspects is evidence which would be sufficient to justify the Home Secretary in banning an organisation or making an exclusion order.

Arrest at ports of entry

Under Sections 12 and 13, the Secretary of State is authorised to confer on examining officers (police, immigration officers, some Customs and Excise officers and, in Northern Ireland, soldiers) powers of arrest and detention. Under these orders officers can 'examine' anyone entering Great Britain or require that arrangements be made for controlled areas at ports.

Under a 1976 Order, private aircraft were required to use designated airports, although no similar provision was made for private shipping.

Operation of the Act

Between 29 November 1974 and 30 September 1980, 4,977 people have been arrested, of whom 642 were held for more than 48 hours. Of these 3,574 were held at ports of entry and 1,403 elsewhere. Two hundred and thirty-two people were served with exclusion orders, 69 were charged with offences under the Act, 20 with conspiracy to commit offences under the Act and 248 with other offences.

Of nearly 5,000 people arrested and detained during the six years' operation of the Acts, the vast majority — 89 per cent — have neither been excluded nor charged with a criminal offence. Of the 1081 people arrested during 1979 and the first nine months of 1980 who were released without charge or exclusion, 193 (18 per cent) were detained for longer than 48 hours, including 29 held for between six and seven days.

In all, only 337 people — 6.8 per cent of those detained — have been charged with criminal offences. Although many of the offences involved were extremely serious — including murder, firearms and explosives offences — the largest single group of charges (65 in all) were theft or similar offences not involving violence. Of the 69 people charged under the Act itself, charges were dropped in two cases and nine people were acquitted. Three were awaiting trial and 55 people were found guilty. Of the 268 charged with other offences, charges were dropped in 23 cases and 27 were acquitted. Forty three people were still awaiting trial when the statistics were published. Of the 175 people convicted, 74 received non-custodial sentences (a fine or an absolute or conditional discharge); 20 were imprisoned for twelve months or less, 22 for between one and five years and 42 for five years or more.

The vast majority of arrests have taken place in Liverpool (1203, 24 per cent), London (1072, 22 per cent) and Dumfries (952, 19 per cent). In all, 72 per cent of arrests under the Act have taken place at ports or airports used by those travelling between Britain and Ireland and Northern Ireland.

The Government's case

These extensive powers of arrest, detention and search are defended on the grounds that they result in convictions which would otherwise not be obtained and that they enable the police to gather information about terrorist activity. The extended period of detention is justified by the need to check on a suspect's identity. Lord Shackleton stated in his report that associates need to be established and addresses verified, and that fingerprinting and photographing or the swabbing of hands or clothes for the traces of explosives 'all takes time'. Furthermore other police forces throughout the United Kingdom, including the Royal Ulster Constabulary, may have to be consulted. Lord Shackleton pointed out how useful the extended period of detention under the Northern Ireland (Emergency Provisions) Act had been to the RUC — although that Act only permits 72 hours detention.

The requirement to obtain the Home Secretary's permission for a further five days' detention is also, in the Government's view, a safeguard. In England and Wales, the police submit a report in writing to the Home Office whose officials advise the Minister of State and the Secretary of State, although where time is exceptionally short, a senior police officer may explain the background to the Secretary of State in person, or if necessary a Minister of State. Lord Shackleton revealed that where a Minister or Secretary of State is not available, authority is granted by a senior official in the Home Office until the Secretary of State can consider the case himself. Only three applications for an extension beyond the initial 48 hours have ever been refused.

Why these powers are unnecessary

The new powers of detention cannot be justified by the need to bring suspects before the courts on criminal charges. Sufficient powers existed before the introduction of the Act to enable the police to do this job. The police may arrest without warrant anyone reasonably suspected of any criminal offence carrying at least five years' imprisonment on conviction, together with over 100 other lesser offences.

The existing common law and statutory rules concerning length of detention are already deplorably vague and therefore permit the police, on occasion, to hold suspects for a number of days. (Although the police are required to bring someone charged with a serious offence before the magistrates court 'as soon as practicable', there is no restriction on the period between arrest and charge). All the people detained under the Act and subsequently charged with criminal offences could have been arrested and questioned without using the detention powers of the Act itself. Roy Jenkins, as Home Secretary, himself admitted this point during a debate on the Act: 'It could be reasonably pointed out that a considerable number of people . . . would have been arrested under normal police powers if the Act had not been in force. What the section does is to strengthen, extend and perhaps in some cases *regularise* police powers of arrest and detention in relation to suspected terrorists' (our italics). After presenting recent arrest figures, he went on: 'Clearly most of these people would have been detained even if the Act had not been in force'.

Neither the arrest and charging of six people following the Birmingham bombings in November 1974 nor of four people after the Balcombe Street siege was affected by the Prevention of Terrorism Act. It is efficient and speedy police work, not emergency powers, which result in suspects being brought to trial.

The Government also admitted that it was possible for surveillance of people at ports of entry to be carried out 'without special statutory powers, as it was before the Act came into force'. But the new powers given to examining officers at ports of entry encourages fishing operations, designed to collect information or simply to intimidate political activists. The case of **Margaretta D'Arcy**, a well-known socialist playwright, is not unusual. She was held on 9 January 1980 and describes her experience thus:

> I was travelling from Belfast to London and on leaving the boat at Stranraer (approx 5.30 pm) I had my luggage searched. Inside my bag were a number of pamphlets about the conditions of the H-block prisoners in Northern Ireland. I was brought to the police station, having been taken to a police office in the dockside railway station. I had already filled in the regular form giving my name, address, journey particulars and business. I was told in the railway police office that I was being arrested under the PTA. At the town police station I refused to answer any questions; stating that this was a violation of the Human Rights Charter to which both Britain and Ireland were signatories. Present were two police officers (one 'nice' and one 'nasty') and a woman 'search-officer'. The 'nasty' one tried to rile me with sexual innuendoes about 'Sabrina's Bra', in reference to women's lib. I pointed out that sexual humiliations were expressly mentioned in the Bennett Report as an improper activity for the police, and he shut up. I had on me copies of the Human Rights Charter, the Amnesty Report and the Bennett Report. If I had not had this documentation, I am sure the 'nasty' policeman would have gone much further in psychological harassment. No more questions were asked me, and I was let go after an hour and a half. I knew no-one in Stranraer and accordingly felt very vulnerable. The entire procedure seemed to have no purpose other than to instill fear into me.

During the 1979 General Election, Labour Party canvassers in the London constituency of Hampstead were arrested uner the Act. **Margaret Fletcher**, a student at Middlesex Polytechnic, and **Nick Mullen**, another student and a member of the Troops Out Movement, were arrested on polling day while 'knocking up' voters. Ms Fletcher was strip-searched and released after a period in the cells, but Mr Mullen was held for a longer period of questioning. It appeared that the officers who arrested them had been watching a flat owned by Paddy Prendeville, a journalist with *Hibernia* magazine in Dublin. As we describe on page 48, Paddy Prendeville was himself arrested under the Act in December 1979.

Many of those detained under the Act are students or political activists travelling between Ireland or Northern Ireland and Britain for conferences. In December 1977, seven delegates to the National Union of Students annual conference were arrested at Blackpool airport, one being held overnight on the grounds of an alleged association with the Provisional IRA. All were released without charge. In June 1978, a Student Community Action worker from Nottingham University was taking a party of young people on a holiday to Nottingham, from Belfast: two of the 16-year-old Catholic boys in the group were arrested, detained for three hours, searched, photographed and fingerprinted. In November of the same year, two students in a party of students and trades unionists visiting Britain for the 'Peace, Jobs, Progress' campaign were detained at the airports in Belfast and Manchester. Like the boys in Nottingham, they complained of police abuse during their period of detention.

In February 1979, **Helen Connor**, then a vice-president of the NUS, was stopped by Special Branch officers at Belfast airport while on union business, and detained for three hours. On her return she was held for a further two hours at Heathrow. She complained that in addition to being searched and fingerprinted by male officers, her documents were photocopied. In December 1979, two members of the Northern Ireland delegation to the NUS conference were detained at Liverpool airport. One of them, **Patricia Clarke**, complained that she was subject to a full body search in front of six male police officers.

In October 1980, **Margaret McNulty**, a delegate from the Republican Clubs (a lawful Republican organisation in Northern Ireland), was arrested at Heathrow airport on her way to a feminist conference in London. Two other women travelling to the same conference were also arrested and detained.

Others have been held when passing through the UK. On 29 October 1979 two men were arrested who were in transit to Holland to work were arrested at Heathrow airport and detained for six days. **Hugh Leekey**, who was arrested on 15 November 1979, had arrived in Liverpool that morning and was due to sign a contract with the Ocean Fleet Line for an eight month contract of work. He was detained for 24 hours, although he claims he was only questioned for 30 minutes. He lost his work and therefore had to return to Belfast.

No safeguards for the suspect

The most objectionable feature of the detention powers is the removal of all safeguards for the suspect. In theory, the Judges' Rules — providing guidelines for police interrogations, including the right of access to a solicitor — apply to detentions under the Act. But the only sanction for breach of the Judges' rule is that, in any subsequent trial, the judge may exclude a statement or confession obtained in breach of the Rules if the result is to make the statement 'involuntary'. The sanction is inadequate at the best of times, since statements obtained in breach of the Rules are regularly admitted in evidence. But it is completely irrelevant in the vast majority of arrests under the Prevention of Terrorism Act, *since the people arrested are never charged or brought to court.*

It is routine practice for the police to deny those held under the Act access to a lawyer. Lord Shackleton considered the problem of safeguards, but noted only that there were considerable variations between police forces, in particular in the way that persons in custody were informed of their rights.

Section 62 of the Criminal Law Act (entitling an arrested person to have someone informed of his arrest and whereabouts) also applies, in theory, to arrests under the Act. But an exception permitting the police to refuse to make notification, if delay 'is necessary in the interests of the police investigation, the prevention of crime or the apprehension of offenders' has ensured that a large number of people arrested under the PTA are held completely *incommunicado*.

Three Irishmen, **Jo Arbuckle, Eugene Barren and Aidan Lofgray**, who worked in Barnsley, went back to Northern Ireland to attend a friend's wedding in May 1980. On their return they were detained by the Liverpool police. No-one was informed. After two days, their Barnsley landlords, concerned at their delay without hearing from them, contacted their families in Northern Ireland.

A Liverpool solicitor agreed to look into the case of their behalf. The police admitted that three men were held, but refused to confirm their identities. Two of the three were subsequently served with exclusion orders (without access to any independent legal advice) and returned to Northern Ireland without making representations. The third was released. No-one was informed of the arrests and no access was given to the solicitor engaged by the men's families.

A further case illustrates that children may be innocent sufferers following a PTA arrest.

In March 1980 **Joe O'Brien** and **Michael Forgione**, together with

Joe's eight-year-old daughter, Elizabeth, were arrested at Liverpool after driving from Northen Ireland across on the ferry to Leyland in Lancashire to collect some of Michael's furniture. On their return, they were arrested on the boat by the Liverpool police, only 15 minutes before the boat was due to leave.

Both men objected about the child and the police informed them that Elizabeth would be sent home by herself. The shipping company refused to take responsibility for her and her father refused to let her go on her own. By this time, Elizabeth was in hysterics having been separated from her father. She asked to be sent to her aunt's home only a short distance away, but was sent instead to the Royal Liverpool Children's Hospital. Her aunt was not informed until 1.30 pm the following day — half an hour before the two men were freed.

No-one in Belfast was informed of the arrests. Joe's wife had gone to the police station to report them missing and only then was told that there had been an emergency on board the boat and her child was in hospital. She was not unnaturally distraught having no further information. When the child and father were reunited they were told to find their own way to the boat.

It is extremely difficult for a detainee to challenge the lawfulness of his arrest and detention by means of an action for false imprisonment. Examining officers at ports of entry — where nearly three-quarters of the arrests take place — are entitled to arrest someone solely on the basis of 'suspicion' of involvement in terrorism. There is no requirement of 'reasonable suspicion' which implies an objective test of the evidence and no court is likely to over-rule the officer's judgment. Inland, however, the arrest must be made on the normal basis of 'reasonable suspicion'. Nonetheless, in only one case — that of Michael Connolly — has an arrest under the Act been successfully challenged.

Michael Connolly, a man with no previous criminal record and little interest in politics, succeeded in obtaining a court order for the destruction of his fingerprints and the record of his arrest under the Act. On 11 October 1977, he and two friends, a West German and an Australian, visited the Old Bailey, having heard on the news that the appeal of the IRA pub bombers was to be heard there.

Because of the IRA court case, special security checks were in operation including body searches at the entrance to the building. The Special Branch had set up an identity check at the entrance to the court, but on the understanding that members of the public who did not want to give their names and addreses should be able to enter any other court. Michael Connolly had no identification with him and knew that his name might cause him difficulties — although he is not Irish. He told his friends he would visit another court and meet them later. The Special Branch officers became suspicious at his disappearance and arrested his friends for refusing to supply his name. Michael Connolly, who was found sitting peacefully in another courtroom, was also arrested even after he had given his name and address. All three were then taken to Snow Hill police station.

Although Michael Connolly had now given his name and address and offered his landlady's name as a source of proof, he was photographed and had swabs taken to check for explosives. He was placed in a cell and told that he could be held for seven days. Uncertain about why he was being held at all, Michael Connolly objected to having his fingerprints taken and asked whether they would be returned or destroyed. He says that he was told he could write to the Police Commissioner, and then gave permission for his prints to be taken. While he was held, his flat was searched by police officers accompanied by dogs. He was released after 7½ hours' detention without, as counsel for the police later suggested, 'a stain on his character'— except for a newly-opened Special Branch file.

NCCL's legal officer represented Michael Connolly in his action for wrongful arrest and an application for an order that the documents, including fingerprints and photograph, be destroyed. The action was successful. The jury decided that because he had not been properly informed of the reasons for his arrest, the arrest was unlawful, and he was awarded nominal damages. More importantly, the judge ordered the destruction of the documents — an order against which the police did not appeal. But Michael Connolly was ordered to pay £180 in legal aid contribution.

Despite the finding in the Connolly case, the police have subsequently refused all claims by other people held under the Act for the destruction or return of the records. Before the case came to court, the then Minister of State, Lord Harris, had told Christopher Price MP that:

> The general principle is that while the powers contained in this Act remain in force, photographs and fingerprints of all persons detained are being retained centrally by the police. Details of persons detained are also kept for record purposes. I am afraid that, as with any such case, I can give no such assurance that Mr Connolly will not be questioned again in the future.

Although the records of Michael Connolly's detention have now been destroyed, anyone else who has once been held under the Act runs the risk of being arrested and detained again simply because the police or examining officers are aware of the earlier incident. The collection and use of information about people who have been detained but released without charge is currently being examined by the European Human Rights Commission in three cases backed by NCCL which have been declared admissible.

Michael Connolly is by no means the only person to be arrested simply because he was near a law court at the wrong time. In September 1975, **'Betty Jones'**, an Irish girl living and working in London, was showing her two sisters from Belfast around London. They parked their car, which had Northern Ireland registration plates, in the NCP car park near St Pauls Cathedral, which they planned to visit. They were quite unaware that the Guildford bombing trial had recently started in the Old Bailey nearby. They returned to find the car the object of a bomb scare. They willingly identified themselves to the police and accompanied the officers to Snow Hill police station to have their identification checked.

All three girls were detained for six days. They claim that their repeated requests to telephone their parents in Belfast were refused. One sister was woken early in the morning and asked to sign her name at the bottom of a blank statement sheet — 'just to provide a sample of your handwriting'! Their parents eventually contacted a Belfast solicitor who in turn alerted a London solicitor. He was allowed to see them the day before they were released. He explained that they were entitled to have food sent in (one of the girls, a vegetarian, had been unable to get suitable food). None of the girls was questioned during their period of detention.

Habeas corpus

In theory, someone held under the Act is entitled to apply for a writ of *habeas corpus*. But this centuries-old remedy against unlawful detention has been nullified by the Prevention of Terrorism Act. By giving examining officers objectionably wide powers of arrest, and by making detention beyond 48 hours lawful with the Home Secretary's consent, the Act makes it impossible in practice to challenge the lawfulness of the detention. In any case, the courts have refused to treat such applications seriously. A habeas corpus application made on behalf of Paddy Prenderville in December 1979 (see page 48) was adjourned for four days!

Although the power to exclude may only be used against those suspected of an involvement in terrorism relating to Northern Ireland, there is no such restriction on the power of arrest and detention. In other words, the Act gives the police the power to arrest and detain anyone suspected of involvement in 'the use of violence for political ends' — a definition vague enough to encompass people involved in a demonstration or picket where violence occurred. At the end of March 1980, during 'Operation Fire' (a series of arrests in Wales connected with arson and attempted arson) one person was arrested under the Act and subsequently charged at Luton, in Bedfordshire, with conspiracy to cause explosions. In reply to Parliamentary Questions for the Plaid Cymru MP Dafydd Ellis Thomas, the Minster of State at the Home Office, Leon Brittan, replied that no information was held about the number of *arrests* made under the Prevention of Terrorism Act which were unconnected with Northern Ireland. He went on to say that the Home Secretary would only grant an extension of the detention period beyond the first 48 hours 'where a connection with terrorism related to Northern Irish affairs is established or suspected' (Hansard, 5 November 1980). But there is nothing in the Act to impose such a restriction and nothing to prevent a change of policy which would permit detention for up to seven days of people entirely unconnected with Northern Irish matters.

European Human Rights Convention

In December 1979, the Human Rights Commission declared admissable three cases brought by people who had been detained under the Act. In making that decision, the Commission accepted NCCL's argument that there is no 'domestic remedy' for alleged violations of the Convention arising from an arrest and detention under the Prevention of Terrorism Act. The Government had argued that the applications were inadmissible since none of the complaints had challenged the lawfulness of their detention by applying in the British courts for habeas corpus or making a claim for unlawful imprisonment.

Two of those who have complained to the Commission are United Kingdom citizens; the third is Irish. On 22 February 1977, the three men arrived in Liverpool on the ferry from Dublin, having been on holiday together in Ireland. They were arrested and detained at a police station in Liverpool for 45 hours before being released without charge. They were searched, fingerprinted, photographed and questioned. They complained that they were not given proper reasons for their arrests, and two said that they were prevented from contacting their wives. The Government denied all the complaints, and said that the police had had information that at least one the men had been involved 'in matters connected with terrorism'. Despite the Government's denials, the complaints were admitted.

The Commission informed the Government and the complainants that it would like to seek a 'friendly settlement' of the complaint. It is, however, hard to see how any such settlement can be achieved as long as the Government persist in its refusal to abandon the Act. It is therefore possible that the case will be referred to the European Human Rights Court.

Forcible fingerprinting and photographing

As illustrated by the Connolly case, all persons held under the Act are fingerprinted and photographed, 'reasonable force' being used where necessary. All photographs and fingerprints will be retained during the lifetime of the Act and are held in the national fingerprint collection at New Scotland Yard. This applies whether or not a person is released without charge or exclusion order. Apart from Connolly, no case is known of a successful application being made to destroy prints and photographs and, despite Connolly, the Metropolitan Police have subsequently refused to destroyed prints taken from someone released without charge.

The danger of such records is that the facts of arrest under the Act will be used in future as grounds of suspicion against that person. It is because an innocent person can be seriously prejudiced by an arrest record even where no charges were brought or no convictions obtained, that such records are not nationally kept in this country. The Act is an unacceptable departure from this general principle.

The effects of extended detention

By allowing suspects to be held in complete isolation in the police station, compelled to submit to fingerprinting, photographing and forensic tests, possibly subject to abuse, intimidation or physical ill-treatment, the Prevention of Terrorism Act considerably increases the risk that the detainee will make a false confession to the police or make false allegations against someone else. The risk is increased with extended periods of detention. William Sargent, author of the seminal study *Battle for the Mind*, has explained that interrogators require six constant factors for 'successful' questioning: fatigue, tensions, isolation, uncertainty, use of vicious language and a permeating atmosphere of seriousness. The Act's provisions and the virtual abolition of all normal safeguards make it impossible to regard as reliable confessions or statements obtained from those detained.

Paddy Prendeville, assistant editor of the Dublin magazine *Hibernia*, gave a vivid account of his arrest and detention at the end of a holiday in London in December 1979.

I never had a gun pointed at me before. But now there were three of them aimed straight at my heart held by three police officers shouting 'Don't move . . . turn around . . . hands against the wall'. As they searched and handcuffed me I noticed that their hands were gloved in polythene material, presumably to avoid fingerprinting the flat. One of them flexed his fingers and clenched his fists mencacingly and his strange gloves only added to the threatening expression on his face as he warned me to stop talking to my companion.

Seconds earlier my friend and I had been squeezing the last few drops out of a whisky bottle. It was 4.15 am, Wednesday, 12 December, and the last night of what had been a very enjoyable holiday. The two thunderous bangs on the door (it had been broken down) were followed by the thump of running feet in the hallway, and three pistol toting men (one in uniform) burst through the living-room door followed by several others.

After the initial mayhem had died down, Detective Inspector Beck announced himself and told us that we were being arrested under the PTA. My protesting friend was told by the only woman police officer present that she would be strip-searched in front of the male officers if she did not shut up. They started to pull her pullover off and then led her into the kitchen.

On the way to Leman Street Police Station my escort who I later discovered had the unlikely name of my childhood football hero, Bobby Charlton — joked with the others as we pased the Old Bailey. 'Want to nip in for a quick plea?' said one; 'It'll be all over in a few seconds', said another. They sniggered, as I protested my innocence with as much dignity as I could muster. Bobby Charlton then asked me how long I had been staying in the flat. When I told him I would answer no questions until I had seen my solicitor he came out with the first of several TV cop cliches that I was to hear over the next few days: 'Just remember sonny boy, it's very easy to slip and fall when you get of this van'. Very reassuring!

Charlton's conversation and my own peace of mind did not improve in the next few hours as he swabbed my hands for traces of explosives (!) and took fingerprints, photos and other details from me. Ridiculing my protestations of innocence of any crime he gravely informed me that in his experience as a policmen 'dealing with the flotsam of society I never believe your kind'.

He asked me if I had any political views and I replied cautiously that I supported the Irish dimension as enunciated by the Taoiseach, Charlie Haughey. This confused him thoroughly. 'Eh? What's a teeshuck? Who's this bloke Awee? Is he head of the IRA then?' He asked me if I had ever been in trouble before and refused to accept my negative reply, saying 'come on, you must have a record, you're Irish'.

The real interrogators were less racialist and definitely less amusing as I was soon to discover. I spent the first 24 hours in a filthy cell, completely naked for the first few hours as all my clothes had been taken off me, but was subjected to no questioning at all. My gloom and self-pity were not relieved by snatches of conversation from the next cell. A Mr Duffy asked why he had been arrested and was told that he was being held under the Prevention of Terrorism Act to which he retorted: 'I'm 67 years of age, how in the name of Jesus could I terrorise anybody?' The conversation ended abruptly with the clanking of cell door, lock and key.

But on the Thursday morning I was led upstairs to an office by two well-dressed members of the Anti-Terrorist Squad (ATS) who proceeded, with chilling efficiency, to administer to me the most terrifying few days of my life. After cursory details of my life and family had been taken they insisted that I had no right to silence.

They dismissed the solicitors I mentioned as hack lawyers who were only interested in money. I was also told that the least I could expect was to be charged under Section 11 of the PTA. I eventually agreed to give details of my movements, starting with the Thursday afternoon when I had landed at London's Heathrow Airport, and so I described in detail the first few hours of my visit. This concluded the third two-hour session of the day and I was led down to my cell.

But that night I thought over my position again. I realised that even my innocent 'alibi', which would include references to dozens of individuals and friends I had met in the last few days, most of them concerned in left-wing politics, could inadvertently place question marks over others and even myself. I determined, whatever the consequences, to answer no more questions.

On the Friday morning they became very threatening and interrogator number one told me that I was definitely linked to the 'hair-raising' events of the last few days which he claimed were even bigger that the exploits of the Balcombe Street IRA unit. 'It would make your hair curl, Paddy', he kept repeating. His number two nodded seriously in agreement. Number one then threw a second bombshell at me: 'We also have evidence to link you with Airey Neave's murder last March!'

I could feel my jaw sag as he started to question me about various political activities in Ireland. The fact that I knew some of those named (as indeed my job requires) appeared to be proof positive in his mind that I was implicated in the two most serious offences of 1979. But more was to come. He leaned over the table into my face and said, 'I told you that you are linked to the two biggest terrorist crimes of the last twelve months; well, I was wrong, you're also involved in a third — the Provo bombs in London last Christmas!' I nearly fainted and he walked over the door. 'Let's bring him down to his cell', he said to number two, 'and I hope your hair does not turn white tonight, Paddy, I bet you don't get much sleep', he added.

He was correct about the lack of sleep. It was now the third night, and since Thursday morning I had been subjected to six sessions of interrogation, each lasting two hours. My feeling of isolation and despair was complete. I remembered a remark by number one about juries being very impressionable. He was warning me that twelve good English men and true would be very impressed by the weight of such allegations no matter how circumstantial or spurious the evidence. I decided to shut up altogether, not only about my visit to London but everything and anything.

The next morning, Saturday, I tried to appear determined as I announced my intention to remain completely silent. I told them that they had terrified me (which was true) by accusing me of several major crimes. As each innocuous answer I had given only seemed to incriminate me, I was saying nothing until I saw my solicitor.

Number one looked quite angry and repeated that I was in it up to my neck. 'A right hornets' nest', he added, 'but I'll tell you what I'll do. If you tell us exactly what we want to know' (he paused and I waited for the offer of a Queen's pardon for offences which I had not committed) 'at end of the day I'll see you fine'. Assuring myself that I would not have accepted any offer (no informer me, not even of fiction!) never mind his ridiculous one, I repeated my adamant intention to remain silent.

They suddenly became very concerned. How could they persuade me that they only wanted to help me? I answered, again truthfully, that they could not. Then suddenly they changed course. They assured me that their main concern was to prove my innocence which they were almost convinced of. They had not really accused me of involvement in the incidents mentioned. The number two (a Scot) assured me that he actually had many Irish friends; they were great people, 'nice and decent just like you Paddy'. I smiled for the first time in four days and number one raised his eyes to the ceiling. He leaned over and told me to seize my self-confidence. 'You're a man, aren't you Paddy. I suppose you would prefer us to beat you; then you could hate us and it would no problems resisting us'.

I was not at all sure about this but decided to agree with him, adding the black lie that I thought they were very civilised. 'Well then', he said, 'why not be straight with us'. I tried to look non-committal and number one asked me if I would like some lunch. My stomach heaved at the thought of any food, but anything was better than this game of poker and so I tried to look as if no more appetising suggestion had ever been made to me and we adjourned.

They were back in a couple of hours with more sweetness and kindness. Would I like a change of clothes that my sister had brought in? There was a toothbrush and paste in the same bag. Would I like to use them. They didn't mention that my sister's parcel was handed in 48 hours earlier. With a whimper of gratitude I accepted the offers and spent about five minutes furiously brushing my teeth for the first time in four days.

Sitting down to our next session I was swamped with kindly offers of coffee, fruit that my sister had sent in ('little angel isn't she', said one) and, absolute luxury, clean underwear. I accepted all the blandishments as gracefully as possible and waited for their next move.

It came in the form of a political diatribe against IRA extremism and an appeal to my moderate sensibilities. I still insisted on remaining silent and there was another long pause. 'O.K!' sighed one, 'bring him down to his cell'.

Ten minutes later they returned to the cell and casually asked me if I would like to go. As calmly as possible I walked to the cell door and, after collecting some personal items at the station sergeant's desk, I was ushered to the two ATS members' car. I declined their offer of a pint (had they discovered the best way to make me talk?) and we arrived at my sister's house at approximately 6 pm.

My sister shot them a venomous glance and with a cheerio they walked into the Killburn evening.

In some cases, extended detention produces a severe psychological reaction. **Bernard Martin** was arrested in Southampton on 12 December 1979 and detained until the 16th, when he was taken to hospital. He discharged himself on the two days later, and was seen the following day by a psychiatrist. According to the account which Bernard Martin gave to the doctor, his house was raided by police and he was arrested at about 4 am. He was taken to the police station, questioned briefly and placed in a cell. From then on he began to experience a series of 'bizarre and disturbing' hallucinations. Martin's doctor said that he had no major previous medical problems and no history of psychiatric disturbance requiring treatment; nor is there any record of his having received psychiatric treatment in Southampton previously. Medical examination showed bruising on the margin of the right eye, one shoulder, and the upper arm. The psychiatrist concluded that Marin had suffered 'from an abnormal mental state of a psychotic kind' and that his symptoms 'are those which it is known can occur when people are kept in conditions of isolation or sensory deprivation. If a person is placed in an unfamiliar setting without his normal social supports and environmental surroundings with irregular meals and artificial light, this clinical picture can result. The anxiety of being kept in police custody is an important additional factor.'

Like many others who fear repeated arrest or harassment, Mr Martin decided not to make a complaint or take legal action.

Arrest after acquittal

We have stressed that the Act allows the detention and/or exclusion of those against whom there is no evidence on which to base a successful prosecution. In April 1981, the Act was used for the arrest and exclusion of someone who had just been *acquitted* of criminal charges. **Robert Storey** was a co-defendant in the trial which followed an attempt to release from Brixton prison Brian Keenan, who was then on remand on a charge of conspiracy to cause explosions (a charge of which he was subsequently convicted). The jury failed to agree a verdict in Storey's first trial for conspiracy to effect Keenan's escape and for possession of firearms; on the re-trial he was acquitted. Immediately Storey was released from custody he was re-arrested under the Prevention of Terrorism Act and excluded.

Access to a lawyer

The Judges' Rules, which apply to arrests under the Act, give the suspect the right to consult a lawyer — although with the proviso that access to a lawyer may be refused if this would impede the investigation. NCCL has received numerous reports from both detainees and solicitors who complain of having been refused access.

The Bennett Committee report, set up following Amnesty International's investigation of alleged brutality in interrogation centres in Northern Ireland, recommended that a solicitor should have access to a suspect in a police station after the first 48 hours detention and subsequently at 48-hour intervals. More recently, the Royal Commission on Criminal Procedure has recommended that anyone detained on suspicion of a 'grave offence' should be visited by a solicitor after 24 hours (although access to his own solicitor could still be refused if the police believe this would hinder the investigation).

The Government has implemented the Bennett Committee's recommendations, with the result that detainees under both the Prevention of Terrorism Act and the Emergency Provisions Act in Northern Ireland are now entitled to see a solicitor after 48 hours. NCCL believes that the powers of arrest and detention provided by the Prevention of Terrorism Act are objectionable and unjustifiable and should be repealed wholesale. But at the very least, people subjected to extended detention in Britain should be guaranteed a right to see a solicitor.

Summary

The conclusion to be drawn from an examination of general police powers and the use to which the Act has been put, is that the actual use is to allow the police to detain and question Irish people, or people who have some connections with Ireland — even where there is no evidence of suspicion of involvement in a terrorist crime. The power to arrest people effectively at random for the purpose of detaining and questioning them for up to seven days is unacceptable in principle and irrelevant to the need to arrest and bring before the courts those suspected of criminal offences.

Withholding information

What the Act Says

Under Section 11, a new provision in the 1976 Act, it is an offence not to pass on information to the police about a future act of terrorism or about people involved in terrorism occurring in the United Kingdom and connected with Northern Ireland affairs. 'Terrorism' is defined as the use of violence for political ends and includes any use of violence for the purpose of putting the public or any section of the public in fear.

A person who has information which he knows or believes might be of material assistance

(i) in preventing an act of terrorism; or
(ii) in catching, prosecuting or convicting a person involved in terrorism commits offences if he fails to pass on the information to the police (unless he had a reasonable excuse not to do so). (In Northern Ireland the information can be passed on to a member of the Armed Forces.)

Maximum penalties: on conviction in the magistrates' court, a fine of £1000 and/or six months imprisonment, or if the case is heard in the Crown Court, an unlimited fine and/or five years imprisonment.

A person can be charged in any place he has visited since the time that he obtained the information.

The police can arrest anyone without a warrant they reasonably suspect of an offence under this section.

The Government's case

This section originated with George Cunningham MP whose arguments the Government accepted. He said: 'the situation in practice is more likely to be that a prosecution is brought against ten people, for example, for a given outrage, two of them being charged with committing the act and conspiring to do it, and the others being charged formally only with conspiracy. It may be that the jury is satisfied that some of the accused did it and some of them conspired to do it. The jury may, on the evidence, be satisfied that those persons knew about it and could have informed the police. I suggest that this is a realistic scenario. As the law stands, the people found to have knowledge but who did not conspire could not be convicted of anything. I suggest that there is a situation which we should remove'.

George Cunningham later argued that a person charged with a substantial offence and/or with conspiracy should also be subject to a charge of 'concealing infomation', thus enabling a jury which did not convict on the heavier charge to do so the lesser one. This is a general practice in Northern Ireland. Cunningham likened this section to a provision that already exists in the Criminal Law Act 1967, whereby it is an offence to accept a bribe for not giving relevant information to the police. Political motivation, he argued, can be as important as financial reward to the potential offender.

Lord Shackleton expressed grave doubts about section 11, both on grounds of principle and about the way it could be used in the course of interviewing. He added 'It has in any case been little used in Great Britain, and the obvious difficulties of proof may be a factor in this respect . . . Section 11 was not thought necessary in 1974. It has an unpleasant ring about it in terms of civil liberties'. He therefore recommended that it be allowed to lapse forthwith.

During the 1979 debate Merlyn Rees, then Home Secretary, concluded that for the time being the section should not be dropped, but added that the position would be reviewed in a year's time. During the March 1980 renewal debate, William Whitelaw stated: 'I have consulted the police, who are firmly of the view that section 11 is an important weapon in the struggle against terrorism . . . Having considered the matter very carefully, I have concluded that section 11 should be retained'. The Act was subsequently renewed with section 11 intact.

The record

Lord Shackleton was right to say that the section had been little used. However in January 1979, following his recommendation and before the next renewal of the Act, the police arrested twelve persons and charged them under this section in January 1979. Figures given in a Parliamentary answer on 24 November 1980 reveal that in all, 13 people had been charged under section 11; one was found guilty; one acquitted; one charge not proceeded with; and ten were still awaiting trial.

The case against section 11

This section represents a dangerous innovation and in conjunction with the police powers of arrest and detention could lead to suspects giving false and misleading information to obtain an early release from police custody.

Under the Emergency Provisions Act, the Army and police have the right to question an individual as to his or her knowledge of any recent terrorist event and failure to answer 'to the best of one's ability' can result in a maximum sentence of six months imprisonment and/or a fine of £100. The power has been widely abused by the Army to carry out the collection of low-level intelligence and census information-gathering, enabling the Army to boast knowledge of wallpaper colouring of every house in certain areas of Belfast! Such information has been used to intern suspects, and of course, under this Act could form part of the exclusion dossier presented to the Secretary of State.

The effect of section 11 is to undermine a suspect's right to remain silent during questioning. For although a detained person has the right to remain silent under questioning, it is a criminal offence not to pass on certain information. As stated previously, the police have on numerous occasions called for the right of a suspect to remain silent to be weakened — although the Royal Commission on Criminal Procedure rejected such a proposal.

The section is so vague that it is impossible to know whether or not an offence has been committed under it. The NCCL firmly believes in the right of a suspect to know the nature of the suspicion which forms the basis of his arrest. The section gives the police the right to arrest a person on the basis of 'reasonable suspicion that they possess information on terrorism'. In practice it is impossible to challenge the nature of this 'reasonable suspicion' and section 11 therefore legitimises fishing-trips by the police to obtain information from people who are not themselves suspected of involvement in terrorism.

The government have justified changes in court procedure in Northern Ireland alleging that potential witnesses were afraid to disclose information about terrorist activity. By creating an offence for non-disclosure many potential witnesses may be pushed into a dangerous and irreconcilable dilemma. As Gerry Fitt MP put it 'his information would be evidence and he would have to appear in court. Moreover he would be a witness for the prosecution and his name and address would probably be made known . . . If they (the terrorists) did not take the informant's life, they could easily intimidate him by attacking his family'.

The NCCL believes that this section has not in practice enabled the police to bring to court the people involved in terrorist activities who would otherwise have gone free. Despite Lord Shackleton's recommendations, the Home Secretary has succumbed to pressure from the police who are clearly delighted that it has now become a criminal offence for a person not to talk to them.

Censorship

Section 11 has also been used by the Government in an attempt to intimidate the broadcasting media. The BBC Television film of a Provisional IRA roadblock at Carrickfergus in 1980 was referred to the Director of Public Prosecutions for consideration of a prosecution under the Act. Although he decided not to prosecute in this case, the Attorney General, Sir Michael Havers, said on 1 August: 'I profoundly disapprove of the conduct of the BBC staff directly involved which was, in my opinion, deplorable'. He promised that the British government would take a tougher line in future with media organisations publishing interviews with terrorist organisations.

The use of the Acts in Northern Ireland

When Roy Jenkins, introducing the Prevention of Terrorism (Temporary Provisions) Bill in the House of Commons in 1974, described it as a 'draconian' measure, he was, of course, referring to its operation in Britain. By contrast, in Northern Ireland, the Bill simply followed the tradition of repressive legislation such as the Civil Authorities (Special Powers) Acts 1922-40 and the Northern Ireland (Emergency Provisions) Act 1973 which the Province had come to accept as commonplace.

Indeed, the main provisions of the Prevention of Terrorism Act were not strangers to the people of Northern Ireland. Under the Special Powers Act, exclusion orders existed in the form of the Minister of Home Affairs having the power to exclude a person from all but a tiny part of the province, thereby effectively excluding him from all of it. Under the same Act the police had the power to arrest and detain for 48 hours; under the Emergency Provisions Act, the police may detain for up to 72 hours and, like the Prevention of Terrorism Act, the detainee need not be suspected of any specific offence. As for the powers of search, seizure, fingerprinting and photographing, almost identical provisions have been in force in Northern Ireland at least since 1973. Even the new offence of withholding information is no innovation: since 1973, it has been an offence to refuse to answer to the best of one's ability when stopped and questioned by the RUC or security forces about knowledge of terrorist activity. The question that must be asked, therefore, is whether the operation of the Prevention of Terrorism Act has brought anything new to Northern Ireland.

Power of arrest and detention

The existence of section 12 of the Act gives the Royal Ulster Constabulary (RUC) a choice over which legislation to use when they wish to interrogate a suspect about involvement in terrorism. If they use section 12 they can hold a suspect for 48 hours and, with the consent of the Secretary of State, for a further five days without charge, provided they have 'reasonable suspicion' of his involvement in terrorism. If they use section 11 of the Northern Ireland legislation, they can only hold the suspect for 72 hours without charge, yet they do not need the consent of the Secretary of State and there is no statutory requirement that their suspicion be reasonable. However, since the Secretary of State has only refused two applications for extended detention out of a total of 605 and since the reasonableness or otherwise of the suspicion has never been challenged to any effect, one might expect the RUC to prefer the section 12 power, which affords them greater freedom in terms of the length of time they have to interview the suspect.

Surprisingly, the statistics reveal a marked preference on the part of the RUC for the section 11 power of the Emergency Provisions Act. Between 1 September 1977 and 31 August 1978, 2,814 persons were detained under the Emergency Provisions Act (72 hour power) and only 156 under the Prevention of Terrorism Act (seven day power). Furthermore, it would appear that the latter is not being used principally for the general purpose of gathering intelligence on and monitoring the movements of Republican organisations and sympathisers, as it would appear to be in Britain, but primarily to bring suspects before the court. Whereas in Britain, only 6.8 per cent of those detained under the Prevention of Terrorism Act have been charged with an offence, in Northern Ireland the equivalent figure is 46 per cent.

The Northern Ireland figure would suggest that when the police make an arrest under the seven-day power it is a deliberate, pre-planned operation in a case where they have a strong suspicion that the person or persons arrested are involved in a number of acts of terrorism and that the questioning and enquiries will necessarily be lengthy. This, indeed, is their official explanation for using the seven-day power as opposed to the three-day power, and in support of their contention they point to the relatively sparing use of the Prevention of Terrorism Act as opposed to section 11 of the Emergency Provisions Act. Further support for their contention is afforded by the fact that of those detained under the PTA, 82 per cent are held for more than the initial 48 hours.

There are, however, other and more disturbing reasons why nearly half of those held under the PTA should eventually be charged compared with about 7 per cent in Britain and 35 per cent in Northern Ireland of all those held under either Emergency Provisions or the Prevention of Terrorism Act. The amended rules on the admissibility of confessions in scheduled offences (those connected with terrorism), making it more difficult to challenge an alleged confession, together with the abolition of juries, has made it much easier for the police in Northern Ireland to secure a conviction for a terrorist offence than is the case in Britain. Furthermore, the interrogation system which operates in Northern Ireland and which has given rise to serious criticisms of brutality means that, despite the reforms introduced after the Bennett report and the changes made by the new Chief Constable, a suspect in an interrogation centre will still be under extreme pressure to make a confession whether it be true or false. There is a greater likelihood, therefore, that the rate of confessions, and so the rate of charges, will be higher for those detained under section 12 of the Prevention of Terrorism Act compared with those under section 11 of the Emergency Provisions Act, as it would be more difficult to withstand the pressure for seven days as opposed to three. Of all those charged after being arrested under the PTA, the vast majority — 92 per cent were held for more than 48 hours.

Recent research by Tom Hadden, Kevin Boyle and Paddy Hillyard, published by the Cobden Trust, revealed that in Northern Ireland over 70 per cent of those suspected of terrorist offences made a statement within the first six hours of interrogation. But the same research also showed that suspects held under the PTA are interviewed for longer periods of time. A study of 31 suspects held under the PTA in Northern Ireland between 1 January and 30 April 1979 showed that over half were interviewed for over 15 hours altogether, compared with only 10 per cent of those arrested under other powers. Of those interviewed, only three made no statement. All 31 were subsequently charged, and in 15 cases the only evidence against the defendant was the statement made during police interrogation. All were convicted.

The following case taken from this research illustrates the extended interviewing which takes place under a PTA arrest.

A 21 year old Republican was arrested at 6.15 am on 8 July and taken to an interrogation centre. Interviewing sessions were recorded over the next five days as follows:

8 July	11.40-13.05	10 July	11.00-12.00
	14.10-15.10		13.25-15.15
	15.35-17.15	11 July	14.20-16.10
	19.30-21.45		16.30-17.15
	22.40-01.35		19.30-21.05
9 July	11.05-13.30	12 July	10.15-11.20
	14.25-17.25		
	18.15-21.30		
	21.50-02.15		

The suspect made a statement admitting membership of an illegal organisation at 18.15 on 9 July. The following day he admitted his part in a kidnapping and other offences: charges for these offences were made on 12 July.

The power of exclusion and detention at the ports

The Secretary of State's power to exclude persons from Britain, Northern Ireland or the United Kingdom would appear at first sight from the statistics to be relatively unimportant in the province. At 31 December 1979 only eight persons had been excluded from the province, all of whom were sent to the Republic. Initially there was no power to exclude from Northern Ireland alone. Power to do this was only granted to appease the loyalist leaders who felt that the province was not being treated as an equal, integral part of the United Kingdom. However the extension of this power has meant nothing in practice, since no-one had ever been excluded from Northern Ireland to Britain.

What is relevant about the power of exclusion in Northern Ireland is the fact that the excluded traffic-flow is entirely one way from Britain to Northern Ireland. Up to 30 June 1980, 192 persons had been excluded from Britain to the North. Roy Jenkins' idle boast that the power of exclusion had enabled him to rid Britain of the most experienced leaders of the Provisional and Official IRA means, in effect, if his claim is correct that he has been able to confine all the potential trouble-makers to Northern Ireland — not a very magnanimous gesture. However, since only one of those sent back to the province has ever been charged with an offence it is doubtful if his description of them is correct. Nevertheless the aim of the exclusion power is quite clearly to purge Britain of all suspected terrorists against whom there is insufficient evidence to convict, even if that means saturating Northern Ireland with more potential terrorists. This is hardly in keeping with successive governments' declared aim of treating the province as an integral part of the United Kingdom.

Northern Ireland also suffers from the power of exclusion in that it is mostly Northern Irish people who are arrested, detained, questioned and excluded from Britain. One case which provoked a considerable reaction was that of the nine Belfast dockers who went to Liverpool on a two-week government training scheme. Although the RUC had given the nine the all-clear they were arrested on arrival at Liverpool and one of them, **Paddy Kelly**, was held for four days and then excluded. Not all the cases, however, take place at the ports of entry. In another (see page 33) a Northern Irish man, married and living in Kent, was arrested and questioned about an offence. He was sent back to Northern Ireland under an exclusion order leaving his wife and two children in Kent.

It is not just the exclusion orders alone which affect Northern Irish travellers to Britain. The powers of arrest and detention at the ports would appear to be used randomly and oppressively against people from the province. In December 1978, 22 men were arrested while boarding the Larne ferry at Stranraer; of these two were held for questioning overnight. Most notorious of all are the Liverpool police. Out of 3,443 detentions at ports up to June 1980, 1,171 or more than one-third, had been effected by the Liverpool police. One of those cases was a young honeymoon couple from Derry who were held in Liverpool for 48 hours. Mr Gerry Fitt MP even found it necessary to complain that the Liverpool police had shown a special zeal in arresting incoming Northerners.

The use of the exclusion powers and the powers of arrest and detention have meant that not only has travel between the province and Britain become an irksome and often unpleasant experience, but that people from Northern Ireland no longer enjoy freedom of movement between the province and Britain. The operation of the Prevention of Terrorism Act, apart from its obnoxious invasions of human rights and privacy, makes a nonsense of the British government's claim that the people of Northern Ireland are equal citizens of the United Kingdom.

Withholding information

By December 1979, 38 people in Northern Ireland had been charged under section 11 of the Act. In many cases it would appear that this charge is used as a last resort when the police have a strong suspicion that the accused was actively involved in a terrorist incident but cannot produce the evidence linking him with the actual incident. The new effect of this is that many people could find themselves behind bars not because they were actually involved in a terrorist incident, but because they knew something about it and the police, but not the court, had a strong suspicion that they were involved in it.

Other provisions

The remaining provisions of the Prevention of Terrorism Act already applied in Northern Ireland from 1973 or earlier. Indeed part I of the 1976 Act (banning of organisations) does not apply to Northern Ireland as its provisions are adequately catered for by the

1973 Act. The only difference is that more organisations are banned in Northern Ireland, the extra ones being Cumann na mBan, Fianna Eireann, the Red Hand Commandoes, Saor Eire, UFF and UVF. The powers of search and seizure and the powers of fingerprinting and photographing a detained suspect are almost identical in both Acts. However, there is one important practical feature about the power to search which is peculiar to Northern Ireland. Throughout most of the 1970s Belfast and all the provincial towns had a security cordon around their town centres. Each individual entering the town centre was physically searched. Now, although all the provincial towns have abandoned their cordons, the public searches still remain. It is not unusual for man, woman or child to be stopped at random by the police or the security forces and physically searched in any of the town centres.

Conclusion

The operation of the Prevention of Terrorism Act varies depending upon whether one lives in Northern Ireland or Britain. In both cases the immediate effect is a 'draconian' invasion of fundamental human rights and freedoms. However, in Northern Ireland its impact is even more severe. The power of exclusion is used exclusively to provide a one-way flow of traffic of alleged terrorists to Northern Ireland; the powers of arrest and detention at the ports are used mainly to harass travellers from the province; the power to prefer a charge of withholding information about acts of terrorism is used in cases where it cannot be proved beyond a reasonable doubt, even in the special courts, that the person was actually implicated in the act of terrorism; the power to search is used on a random basis to subject individuals to embarrassing, physical searches in public; and, finally, the power of arrest and detention for seven days when combined with the special courts, special interrogation centres and special rules of evidence means that it is much easier for the police to obtain confessions from suspects and then secure their conviction.

In Britain, the Act is used primarily to obtain information and to punish people — through detention or exclusion — without bringing them before the courts. Within Northern Ireland, the Act is part of a system of emergency powers extending to the courts themselves, designed to obtain confessions through interrogation as the basis of conviction and imprisonment.

Conclusions

The Prevention of Terrorism Acts have severely undermined the principles of natural justice and the rule of law. Their provisions violate international standards on human rights — standards accepted by the British Government itself. The following points summarise the most disturbing effects of the Acts.

1. By giving the Home Secretary the power to authorise detention for up to seven days without access to a court, the Act has destroyed *habeas corpus* as a safeguard against unlawful detention.
2. The Act authorises detention for questioning. A detainee need not be suspected of any specific offence: arrest and detention can be based on 'reasonable' suspicion of involvement in 'terrorism' generally. For detention at ports of entry — where the majority occur — the suspicion need not even be 'reasonable'.
3. The power to exclude a United Kingdom citizen from one part of the country to another has given the Home Secretary the right to impose arbitrary, executive punishment on the basis of secret evidence. The suspect has no right to know or challenge the evidence against him and no right to a court hearing. The exclusion order provision is probably a breach of the European Human Rights Convention (which guarantees the right to a fair hearing); furthermore, its continued existence makes it impossible for the United Kingdom to ratify Protocol 4 of the Convention (which protects the right of citizens to freedom of movement within their own country).
4. The power to ban organisations by executive decision, coupled with vague provisions about support for proscribed organisations or for terrorism generally, severely undermine freedom of association and freedom to express views which conflict with Government policy.

Like the Special Powers Acts, the Prevention of Terrorism Act means that 'individual liberty is no longer protected by law, but is at the arbitrary disposition of the Executive'. Protests from the

United Kingdom about human rights violations abroad come ill from a government which demands such excessive powers for itself. The United Kingdom Government and the British press and large sections of the British public condemned the Soviet Government's 'internal exile' of Sakharov and other dissidents. But a system of internal exile is precisely what the Prevention of Terrorism Act has created for the United Kingdom.

Appendices

Summary of the operation of the Acts in Great Britain, 29 November 1974-31 December 1980

1. *Detentions under the Acts*

Total detained	*At port/ airport*	*Elsewhere*	*Exclusion order made*	*Charged with offence*	*Not charged or excluded*	*Not charged with offence*
5061	3636 (71.8%)	1425 (28.2%)	240 (4.7%)	339 (6.7%)	4482 (88.6%)	4722 (93.3%)

2. *Detentions under the Acts: by police force area*

Metropolitan Area	1091
Merseyside	1221
Dumfries and Galloway	981
Other (England and Wales)	1518
Other (Scotland)	250
Total	5061

3. *Exclusion orders*

Exclusion order applied for	*Orders refused*	*Orders made*	*Person removed to:* N. Ireland	*Person removed to:* Republic	*Person removed to:* Already outside GB	*Revoked before removal*
303	37	266	209	36	10	11

4. *Extension of detention period*

	1979	*1980*
Less than 2 hours	53	20
2 hrs and less than 4	67	34
4 hrs and less than 8	72	25
8 hrs and less than 12	39	22
12 hrs and less than 24	121	92
24 hrs and less than 36	121	121

Total under 48 hours	*560*	*394*
2 days and less than 3	71	22
3 days and less than 4	27	11
4 days and less than 5	14	10
5 days and less than 6	8	7
6 days and less than 7	21	6
7 days	3	1
Total 48 hours or more	*144*	*57*
Total detained but not *charged or excluded*	*704*	*451*

NB: These figures do *not* include people charged with an offence or served with an exclusion order, who are more likely to have been held for over 48 hours.

Persons charged with offences (other than offences under the Prevention of Terrorism Acts) following detention in Northern Ireland under the Acts, 29 November 1974-31 December 1979.

Charge	*No.*
Murder	118
Attempted murder	40
Explosive offences	70
Firearms offences	67
Conspiracy to cause an explosion	13
Conspiracy to murder	9
Membership	70
Burglary	1
Robbery	6
Offences against the person	5
Possession of documents	11
Theft	8
Hi-jackings	9
Malicious damage	1
Illegal processions	1
Unlawful imprisonment	15
Withholding information	8
Intimidation	1
Arson	1
Conspiracy to pervert justice	14
Kidnapping	3
Placing hoax bombs	1
Total	472

Persons detained in Northern Ireland under the Acts, 29 November 1974-31 December 1979.

Year	*Persons detained*	*Extension of detention granted*
From 29 Nov. 1974	0	0
1975	8	5
1976	246	202
1977	162	123
1978	155	144
1979	162	126
Total	733	600

Altogether 605 applications for extensions were made during the period in addition to the 600 granted, two were refused and three withdrawn. In 16 cases the period of extension was less than five days.

The National Council for Civil Liberties has campaigned since 1934 to defend and extend freedom of speech and expression, and to protect the rights of individuals and minorities to equal treatment under just laws. NCCL advises people on their rights; takes cases to courts and tribunals; lobbies Parliament and Government through an all-party Parliamentary Civil Liberties Group; publishes pamphlets about people's rights; and organises campaigns for law reforms. Funded solely by subscriptions and donations, NCCL is the largest independent organisation working for human rights in the United Kingdom.

You can get further details of individual membership or affiliation by organisations or groups from NCCL, 186 Kings Cross Road, London WC1X 9DE.